MW01232784

ISBN: 9798370999413

Convicted Pressure

Instagram: @Dominica.Sharda
Snap Chat: IamTheG.O.A.T
Facebook: fb.me/Dominica.Sharda
Tik Tok: @iam_theGOAT

DEDICATION

This book is dedicated to my one and only, the love of my life.... *Scott E. Hughes III*. Son, I love you with all that I am and without you I wouldn't be the woman that I am. Thank you for loving me unconditionally and inspiring me to be the best version of me. To see you grow has been a blessing. I want you to continue to be the best man you can be. Our talks are everything. I have total trust that you will go out in the world and make your own way. You are one of the strongest individuals I have ever known. You are everything a mom could ever ask for in a son. Continue to be great SON and know that Momma loves you more than ANYTHING in this world!! You already know that I am ALWAYS praying for you, and I will FOREVER have your back!

THANK YOU

I want to give thanks and praise to God. Lord, thank you for choosing me as your daughter and loving beyond life. Lord, you knew the plans you had for me. Plans to prosper me and not harm me. Plans to give me hope and a future. From the moment I was born, my life was planned out and I am thankful because I know you don't make any mistakes.

I want to thank My Grandma Lo for never giving up on me. Thank you for all your love and support. In the worst time of my life and you were there for me. I hope that I can make you proud. I love you and I am forever thankful for you.

Aunt Meka, my girl, you are the reason that my son & I have the relationship we have now. Single handedly you ensure that no matter how much time I was doing in prison, I would have a relationship with my son. For this, I am and will be forever grateful. I love you beyond words and I appreciate you.

To the two people that were my best friends first Nyesha, and our little big sister, Toya. Toya, you have grown to be an amazing mother and for this I admire you. Your children are so amazing and have loved me unconditionally since the first day I came home. Your family welcomed me and Scott into your home and I appreciate you all. I love you and I will always be there for you all. Ny, I love you with all my heart. I know that my incarceration affected you in so many ways and hurt more than anything. But thank you for holding on, coming to visit me and being strong. I love you and I love all your children. We are forever locked in.

To my brother Randy. You know the vibes. You were my first brother, my protector, and you will always be my FAVORITE. I love you and appreciate you, my baby.

Cypress (*We All We Got*) We locked in forever Family.

Thank you to the Felony Girls for all your support. If one win, we all win.

To my parents. . . I love y'all because without y'all there would be no me. Dad, I'm like your first-born son, you Junior. We both love cars, and we are growing in a whole nother direction when it comes to this car game. Thank you for being a part of my life. I am your daughter and no matter what I need you and I appreciate you. Mom, my baby, I LOVE YOU. We went through a lot and what I love most about you is you always gone make a way. A HUSTLER by heart. I love you, honor you, and respect you. You saw greatness in me before anyone else did. Thank you for being my mom.

To My GLOW (Girls Loving Our Wisdom) girls. I love you all. You all have given me another purpose in life and move over you all have pushed me to continue to give my best and my all to life. Thank you to all my LITTLE SISTERS.

To Kiarra B. Thank you sis for putting up with me and helping make all this possible.

To my BFF Tiff Gill, My God sent sister Mary K, and my lifetime friends Daniel E., Mary Wind, and Chanika Moore, thank you.

To the many people that came into my life; maybe it was a reason, a season, or a lifetime. Perhaps you were a teacher, a school mate, a prisoner, a MDOC staff member, or volunteer. Thank you for the impact that you had on me and thank you for helping me to become the woman I am today.

PROLOGUE

"In and out girl! We're going to be in and out."

"You said in and out! What happened to in and out?" I screamed frantically.

Drenched in sweat, I jumped out of my sleep. Every time I closed my eyes to sleep, I dreamt about the robbery.

Glancing over at the clock, I noticed it was only 6:27am. This made the third time I had awakened before my alarm was set go off. Kissing Lil' Scott, my infant son, on his forehead before crawling out of bed, I decided to go get me a glass of water and check my phone. On the list of missed calls was my cousin, Mary, who was more like my sister. We grew up together and were so close that we had our kids two weeks apart. Once I made it back to my room, I decided to give her a call back.

"What's up Sis? Everything good?" She answered the phone with a groggy voice. You could tell that she was sound asleep prior to my call.

"Yes, I'm fine. Just tired as hell. I cannot stay sleep to save my life. Scott is still sleeping though." I smiled as I glanced over at my baby boy.

"Awww girl. You're still shaken up. I mean you were a victim of a robbery not even a week ago. That's some scary shit and not some shit you just get over. Make yourself some hot tea and try to relax though. Girl, I'll be over there in a . . ."

"It's not that." I cut her off. "I've been thinking about Lil' Scott a lot. I can't wait until I am able to move him away from Kalamazoo and provide him with a better life. You know? I just want to be a great mom."

"Girlllll! You are already a great mom. Stop over thinking and overwhelming yourself for nothing." Mary responded. She always knew what to say. Even in the worst times, she was always there to encourage me. Lil Scott and I were staying at my grandmother's house and though there was comfort inside the house, I feared raising my son in this city. There was no doubt in my heart that I needed to move my son to a safer environment so that I would be able to offer him more. He deserved that and I was going to give it to him. "Why'd you get quiet? What's on your mind Sis?" Mary asked concerned, snapping me from my thoughts.

"My bad sis. I was dozing off. Let me try to get some more sleep while Lil Scott is sleep and I'll call you once we both get up."

"Okay. Please try to rest. Lil' Scott is going to be fine. He has a strong Mommy that is going to make sure of that. Don't worry yourself crazy. You better know I got your back too."

"I know."

"Okay. Call me when you get back up."

"I will."

We hung up and I snuggled back up in the bed with my baby. Being silly, I sung him Mario's 'Let Me Love You' until he dozed off. *Ringgg! Ringgg! Ringgg!* I hurried to quiet the alarm so that it would not awaken my baby. It seemed like as soon as I laid down, my alarm went off. My day was already planned so it was no need of complaining. Mary was coming to take us to Big Scott's house. I figured maybe a change of scenery may help me sleep a little better. Our clothes were already laid out last night after I got Lil Scott to sleep in order to save some time this morning. Becoming a mother taught me how to utilize my time more effectively. I hurried to the bathroom to jump in the shower and brush my teeth while Lil Scott was still sound asleep. I made sure to pack enough stuff because we were staying a few days.

A few days turned into weeks but there was no improvement to my sleep pattern. However, I did feel a little more relaxed; especially as time went by. Big Scott was a great help with Lil Scott so that may have been why I was able to manage dealing with the nightmares and the lack of sleep. For the duration of our stay, I remained inside the house. This day was no different. We decided to order take out and watch movies. After the food arrived, I flipped through the channels to find something to watch and stumbled upon the news.

Breaking News! There have been new developments in the fatal robbery at Circle K less than a month ago that resulted in the death of the store's long time Store Manager, Michelle Ortiz. Kalamazoo Police say they already have 2 . .
.

My baby daddy snatched the remote from me and changed the channel.

"Stop! Why would you do that?" I said annoyed.

"You already can't sleep! You don't need to be listening to that shit anymore! Let the police do their job. They gon' catch them niggas." He said sincerely.

"I wish it was that simple." I whispered.

"What you say?"

"Nothing. Let's just find a movie." I needed a refreshing distraction.

The next day I decided that I was going to take Lil Scott to see Grandma. I talked to Grandma every day while I wasn't home but she wanted to see Lil Scott so I promised I would come home for a day or two. I got us both dressed before waking Big Scott from his nap. Between waking up with me at different hours of the night and helping care for Lil Scott, he tried to rest when he could.

"Sharda, you can't wait until tomorrow?" Big Scott asked me as he yawned, obviously tired. Most of family, friends, and people in the neighborhood called me by my middle name, Sharda.

"I don't really want to. I didn't bring a lot of clothes. I know I wash them, and I don't really go anywhere. I'm just ready to go home for a couple days." I responded. He was hesitant at first but eventually obliged. In the car, I bopped my head to the music as we cruised across town.

Approaching Grandma's house, I noticed that there were almost 40 cop cars on the block and police officers on feet everywhere, blocking us from entering the block on

Lawrence Street, so Big Scott pulled around back to Florence Street.

"Damn! Somebody's house is getting raided!" I said and shook my head.

"Hell yeah." He responded as he parked the car and helped me get Lil Scott and our bag out the car. "Want me to walk you to the door?" He asked.

"I'm good." I answered. After he gave Lil Scott a kiss, I made my way up the steps to the house. Juggling Lil Scott and my bags, I unlocked the door before turning to wave goodbye to Big Scott from the doorway. In that moment, I didn't know how literal my goodbye would be.

As soon as I stepped completely inside the house, I dropped my bag and breathed a sigh of relief. It felt good to be home. I was looking forward to chilling with my family to get my mind off things. Grandma's house was dysfunctional, but we were family no matter what. Before I could make it out of the kitchen, Aunt Meka came and blocked the kitchen's entryway while motioning her hands as if she was instructing me to stay back. I was out of breath and in no mood to play around before I could have a seat.

"Auntie, if you don't stop playing so I can lay this heavy baby down." I giggled as I pushed pass her playfully. My laughter was short lived.

"Dominica Sims. . ." A white police officer asked as he rudely pushed pass Grandma and entered the house. He looked down at a picture and back up to me.

"Yes." I responded softly.

"Who the fuck do you think you are pushing pass me into my house? You know I don't fuck with da police! What the hell you done got yourself into?" Grandma asked furiously. "I know you had something to do with that shit."

"We have a warrant for your arrest. You're going to have to come with us." He said sternly. My world stopped spinning for a few seconds. My mind went blank, and I could feel my heart in the pit of my stomach. I asked the officer if I could hug my baby as I knew it would be a long time before I would hug him again. He responded yes and I held my baby close to me tightly as a single tear slid down my face.

"Mommy will be back baby. I promise you." I whispered as I kissed his face before handing him to my big sister, Ny.

"Get a fucking female officer in here. Don't put your fucking hands on her." Aunt Meka yelled but the officers paid her no mind. My sister and my nephew were crying on the floor with fear written all over their faces. The entire scene was chaotic. One officer stood guard to my family while the other read me my rights.

"Dominica Sims, you know exactly what you did. Now, you have the right to remain silent. Anything you say can and will be used against you in a court of law. You have the right to an attorney. If you cannot afford an attorney, one will be provided for you. Do you understand the rights I have just read to you?"

"Yes." I responded. Seeing that my family was already under distress, the officers offered to take me outside before they would cuff me. As they drug me out the door, I could hear Grandma cussing and praying.

"I knew her ass was up to no good! Please help her Lord! Help her Lord please! Only you can save her Lord" Grandma cried out. As the officer led me down the steps, I thought to myself. *GOD, do you find me worth saving?*

pres•sure
/'preSHer/

noun
1. continuous physical force exerted on or against an object by something in contact with it.
2. the use of persuasion, influence, or intimidation to make someone do something

When is the first time you felt like you were under pressure? It's likely that it was probably at birth. As soon as we entered this world, people began to project their perceptions onto us – both the people who had never walked a block in the shoes we would fill and the ones who had lived right door. The pressures you face in your adolescent and teenage years is critical to who you will become as an adult. That's not to say that the trials and tribulations of your experiences will only breed failure and mistakes. It is to say that how you handle the people or circumstances that pressure you and the principle and morale – or lack thereof – that you develop as a result of your experiences, forms your perception of yourself, your surroundings, and the world and how you see yourself in it. What has the pressures of life taught you about yourself?

CHAPTER ONE

In the state of Michigan, 5.5% of all individuals incarcerated are women. This may seem like a small percentage but in no way, shape, or form is incarceration a small or easy experience to get through, especially as a woman. Although most of the things you may hear about prison and incarceration are not true and are mostly fragments of people's imagination, one fact that does not waiver is that prison changes you. It will either change you for the better or for the worse. I know because it changed me. Through my incarceration, I transitioned. I grew wiser and stronger; mentally, physically, and spiritually. All that I knew to be reality, changed. I have been asked on numerous occasions about my experiences in prison. In fact, it may be the question I am asked the most these days. Some people cannot phantom how a female my age could have survived prison and came home with my head held high – primarily because I was sentenced to so much time at such a young age.

Now, I know you may desire to read about the prison tales and learn more about the woman I have become because of my incarceration, and you will. Prison was hard – I will never refute that – but I had spent my entire life learning how to navigate difficult situations. In prison, I was forced to face things that did not bring me comfort. However, it was the morals and principles I was taught as a young girl that helped me survive. So, when people meet me, often they ask me about the things I have encountered and witnessed while incarcerated so that they can live vicariously through my experiences. My response is always, *"Do you have time to listen?"* because the story did not start when those iron gates locked close behind my back. Oh no. In order to understand who I am, how I survived my incarceration, or the impact that prison had on my life and the lives of those who love me, you have to know my story – and that started the day I entered this world.

Grandma Lo, my father's mother and the matriarch of the family, raised me as my mother and father were both incarcerated at different points in my life. We lived in the projects, The Row Houses on Florence. Also living there was my older sister, Ny, whom she also raised, and periodically, my two uncles, Terry and Dirt. What bonded us more than Grandma's love was the fact that we faced our struggles together. Our camaraderie was unmatched. For instance, one day when I was about 5 years old, Ny and I were playing around in the living room while Grandma was cooking. It was a normal day until the police banged on our door. *Bang! Bang! Bang!* The banging startled us.

"Kalamazoo Police! Open up!" One officer shouted. *Bang! Bang! Bang!* "Open this door or we will kick it in." They shouted as they proceeded to bang on the door. Peeking through the blinds, I noticed that the front was surrounded with cop cars and about seven of them were on our front.

"Wait a minute!" Grandma yelled as she came from the kitchen and walked towards the door. "Don't come banging on my fucking door and think I'm going to stop doing with the fuck I'm doing and rush to open it up. Y'all wait until I get to the door." Ny and I ran out the front door as soon as the police kicked the door open knocking Aunt Meka down.

"Ma'am we have an arrest warrant for . . ." Neither of us made out the name but we could hear someone yelling, "She's pregnant! She's pregnant!"

A police officer spotted us running and started chasing us. When we got to my aunt's house, we banged on the door just as the police had just done ours.

"Aunt Bell! Aunt Bell, the police are chasing us!" I shouted. She answered and we were able to slip past her into her home just before the officer reached her steps.

"Umm! Excuse you!" Aunt Bell said as she stepped outside to address the officer while closing her door behind her. "Why are you chasing my nieces?"

"Ma'am, those two girls were just at a house that we are currently raiding with a search warrant. I'm going to need you to order them to come out here now." He demanded as we listened behind the door.

"Who are you searching for?"

"Huh?" The officer asked confusedly.

"The warrant. Who is the search warrant for?"

"Anthony Gester."

"Anthony Gester." Aunt Bell repeated. "Does either of those girls look like the man you are looking for, Mr. Anthony Gester?"

"No, but you could be . . ."

"I could be what? Hiding him?"

"Why, yes, that is a possibility."

"Well, I do not know anyone by the name of Anthony Gester and surely am not hiding no damn body in my house. But I'll tell you what, you run on downtown and get yourself a search warrant for this address and I will let you come in and look for yourself. Until then, you have yourself a good day."

"We'll be back!" He responded defeated as he made his way back to Grandma's front.

"See you then." Aunt Bell smiled and waved. One thing about our family, right, wrong, or indifferent, we had each other's backs no matter what. "Now, what in the world is going on?" She asked us as she closed the door.

"I don't know TT. We don't know anybody names Gester, Lester, or whatever he said." I responded and I really didn't.

"Well, why did y'all run?"

"The police knocked on the door." We said in unison. While the police's job is to protect and serve the communities in which they are employed, I can count on one hand how many times I've seen that occur where I'm from. However, I would need my hands, your hands, and another set of hands too to tally the countless times I have witness police officers harass, bully, and brutalize said communities while hiding behind their badges. It's like their badges somehow gave them the right to shake our entire world upside and they did every chance they got; including when they raided our house with a search warrant. My family did not know nor had never been associated with anyone by the name of Anthony Gester, but we were still forced to vacate our home according to Kalamazoo Housing Department. Crazy, right? Like the police couldn't possibly have had the wrong address.

Nevertheless, Grandma found a place for me, her, and Ny to stay, a shelter for women with children, called The Gospel Mission. It was not home but it was bearable until we got on our feet. The parents attended the classes and trainings required by the shelter to secure housing. After school, the children were responsible for completing our daily chores which were designed so that the center would stay clean. The kids were pretty cool, and I had grown close to Ricky, another kid that stayed at the center with his mom, Barbara. She was there to save her and her kids from an abusive, domestic situation. I thought that was strong of her. A lot of women weren't able to escape the grips of their abusers. He was a couple years older than me, but we clicked almost instantly. He reminded me of my homeboys around my way. That was until one day our connection changed.

We were both assigned to cleaning the kitchen for chores one week and I was exhausted after cleaning it. You would have thought since it got cleaned daily and it was two of us cleaning that we would run through it but that was not the case. We got it done though. We both sat at the kitchen table laughing, joking, and sharing stories about the neighborhoods we were from. Until Ricky jumped up and said he wanted to show me something cool he found in the shelter. I was hesitant as I didn't want Grandma to come looking for me and I was somewhere I had no business being. I knew how important the shelter's help was to us securing a new home and I didn't want to mess that up, but I also trusted Ricky.

"Come on!" Ricky persisted. I sighed and followed him to what looked to be a secret closet in the pantry. There was a bench in there where Ricky took a seat.

"Okay. You showed me. Now, let's go." I said as I got an eerie feeling.

"Naw. Come sit down with me." He said and gently grabbed my arm. Reluctantly, I took a seat. We sat there for a minute in awkward silence. Breaking the awkwardness, Ricky leaned in and kissed me then backed up looking at me. My facial expression was blank as my puzzled brain thought about our friendship. I looked at Ricky like a big brother and thought that he had viewed me same. As these things went through my head, his hand went up my skirt breaking me from my thoughts.

"What are you doing? Stop!" I said and backed away.

"Shhhh! It's going to feel good. Watch." Ricky smiled but I did not as he proceeded to finger me.

"Ouch! Stop! That hurts!" I pleaded with tears rolling down my face. Ricky pulled his fingers out of me, and we both looked at his fingers. They had blood on them, my blood. As I got up and attempted to run pass, Ricky grabbed my arm.

"Don't you tell anyone about this ever." He said with the coldest look in his eyes. That was the last day I ever spoke to Ricky. In fact, I played sick to avoid seeing him or having any kind of contact with him moving forward. My five-year-old brain could not comprehend why my friend would want to violate me in such a way.

Shortly after that incident, through the resources of the shelter, Grandma was able to secure a house for us, a new home of our own finally! We packed our belongings into bags and boxes. I couldn't wait to move out. On our way out the door, Ms. Barbara and Ricky appeared to express their well wishes. It was the first time I had seen Ricky in a couple weeks, and I couldn't stand to look at him. I continued out the door with the bags I was carrying and did not bother to acknowledge Ricky or Ms. Barbara. Once I was finished loading the bags into the vehicle, Grandma and Ny were approaching.

"What's been going on with your ass? I did not raise you to be rude. You know better than that." Grandma started. "And why you ain't say goodbye to your friend Ricky? Y'all used to be joined at the hip." I just continued to ride in silence. We finally had some good news, a new home. I just wanted us to enjoy it. Ricky, that shelter, and everything it entailed was a part of my past and that's exactly where it was staying.

CHAPTER TWO

We settled into our new home in a new neighborhood, and it was all good for the most part but, you know with a new neighborhood comes a new school. At first, I was nervous about what this new chapter would bring for me. Looking in the mirror, I hated how Grandma had dressed me and I immediately started to fix myself. I just wanted to make a good impression on the students at my new school and build some lasting friendships. However, the kids at the school were rude and mean. It felt like I was living in an alternate reality because the experience was nothing like my old school. It was only elementary school so I couldn't imagine what could make the kids so mean. I didn't really spend too much time thinking about it either. Day in and day out, I came to school, did my work as assigned, played along, and went home. That was my routine.

One year, we had a candy fundraiser, and the prizes were dope, so Ny and I wanted to win. We planned out all of the people we were going to ask and what streets we wanted to walk down. Things didn't go as planned though. The thing about school fundraisers is that most of the kids in the school live in the same neighborhood so the customer base was the same. It was disappointing but thankfully Grandma didn't like the idea of going around asking anybody to buy our candy, so she bought both of our boxes. We really didn't have it like that, so I was grateful that Grandma made the sacrifice. The day after we turned the money in, I crossed my fingers as they announced the winners over the intercom. Though I wasn't surprised when they called my name, I couldn't wait to go home and tell Grandma. When Ny and I got in from school, Grandma shushed us because she was on the phone. That's all she was sit on the phone and gossip with her old friends. We sat down at the table and pulled out our books to complete our homework. I danced a little while pulling the prize sheet from my back pack as well. I hadn't decided what I wanted but I was going to make my choice today. Grandma wrapped up her call as Uncle Terry came in the house.

"Uncle Terry, guess what?" I jumped up with my paper.

"What?" He asked sternly. He was always mean, but I wasn't letting him take my joy today.

"I turned in the most money in my grade for the fundraiser, so I get to choose a prize in this section." I told him as I pointed to the paper.

"You ain't sell shit so I don't know what the fuck you're so excited about like you went outside door to door or some shit. That shit still sitting over there on the counter." He responded and I instantly regretted sharing my good news with him.

"Shut the hell up Terry." Grandma said. "Your ass ain't sell that shit when you were in school either."

"Grandma, let me show you. . ." I started but she held her one finger up signaling for me to give her a minute.

"Where is that candy money?" Grandma asked.

"I turned it in. I had the most money in my grade. That's why I am able to choose. . ."

"Shut up. I'm not talking to you. Her raggedy ass knows exactly who the fuck I'm talking to." Grandma said and I followed her eyes to Ny. Once I thought about it. I realized that I didn't hear Ny name as a winner in her grade. "Where the fuck is my money and why didn't you take your ass to school yesterday?" Ny put her head down but remained silent.

"Are you fucking deaf, or you don't hear my mother talking to you?" Uncle Terry yelled at Ny so loud that I jumped. For a few seconds, the room grew so quiet that you could hear a pin drop.

"I'm only going to ask one more time. Where the fuck is my money?" Grandma asked through gritted teeth. Ny's silence irritated Uncle Terry and he directed me to go in the living room. It seemed like as soon as I stepped foot in the living room, I heard Ny scream so loud.

"You want to steal money? You didn't hear my mother talking to you? You wish you turned that fucking money in now, don't you?" Uncle Terry shouted those questions and more as he beat her with a leather belt. It hurt me to hear her scream out in pain so I couldn't help but to cry as well.

"Get the fuck up and go finish your homework." He said as he walked pass me in the living room. I did as I was told and took a seat next to Ny at the dining room table. Pulling her close to me, I comforted her by holding her and rocking back and forth. Scanning her body as she continued to cry, I noticed that some of the welts that she incurred from the whipping had split open and were bleeding. "Shut that fucking crying up before I really give you something to cry about." Uncle Terry shouted from a distance.

"Shhhh!" I whispered to Ny. We cried most of that night. The next day, it was hard for Ny to move but she managed to get dressed. Ny's teacher reported her to the nurse for an exam when she noticed evident bruises and the open welts on her arms. As a result, Child Protective Services made a case against Uncle Terry, and he was sent to prison as a result.

When Thanksgiving break came, not only was I excited to have a few days away from school but to be around my family also. My dad was currently tethered to Grandma's house so whenever he wasn't on the phone handling business, I got to spend a little time with him, and I loved that. My mom was had just come home but she went and got my baby sister, Toto, who at the time was staying with Grandma Hattie, my mom's grandmother, and they moved to Detroit. Now, I did feel a bit neglected because she didn't take me and Ny to live with her, but I was grateful that I had a relationship with her.

My family all came together and cooked a large spread for Thanksgiving dinners, so it was tradition for my family to come together at Grandma's house the night before Thanksgiving to prep the food. Just like any other year, my family was seasoning the dinner meats, mixing salads, dicing onions and peppers, cutting up cheese for the macaroni, saturating the ham and turkey, and preparing everything so that the next day it would just have to cook. Another tradition was me helping Aunt Meka make her famous banana pudding.

"Oh, my goodness! Guess what?" Aunt Meka shouted and startled everyone.

"What's wrong?" Grandma asked. I looked at her anticipating the answer as well. Even Ny peeked her head in the kitchen.

"I forgot to put the bananas in the pudding" We all burst into laughter. "Oh well, it still tastes delicious."

"It definitely does Auntie." I replied while eating a spoonful.

"Yes, baby. We did that!" She said and did a little dance.

Thanksgiving dinner was fun and exciting per usual. Everyone laughed, sang, and had a good time together. We all sat down at the dinner table to eat but my dad stepped away from the table to take a call so I decided that I would wait until he came back to eat.

"Sharda, why are you eating?" Grandma asked.

"Yeah, what's your problem?" Ny added.

"I'm going to eat. I'm just waiting for my dad to come back."

"Well, you go ahead and wait but Aunt Meka is going to enjoy this food." Aunt Meka said with a light laugh as she stuck her fork in her food. My dad came back shortly after, and we enjoyed our food as well. After we ate dinner, everyone went back to chilling and talking. Ny and I were watching TV when the phone rang. Grandma answered the phone.

"Ny! Sharda! Come get the phone. It's Tanya." Tanya is our mom. We both rushed to get the phone. Ny was able to grab it first, but she didn't have a good grip, so I snatched it from her.

"Hey Ma!" I said but Ny took the phone from me before she could respond. "Give me the phone!" I yelled

"Hey Mommy!" Ny sang into the phone receiver teasingly.

"Y'all raggedy asses better cut that shit out or I'm going to make y'all hang up my damn phone!" Grandma yelled from the kitchen.

"Ight!" We both replied in unison. I decided to go ahead and let Ny talk without bothering her because I'd get to talk second and longer. Once she wrapped up her conversation, I got the phone and sat down.

"Now like I was saying Ma. . ." I said and rolled my eyes playfully at Ny. "Heyyy. What you doing Ma?"

"I'm not doing much right now girl. What are you doing? Are you enjoying Thanksgiving?"

"Yes, but I want to come over there with you."

"Ooouuu! Yes Ma, can we come over there?" Ny yelled towards the phone. I screwed my face up with irritation. "You had your turn. Can I talk?" She rolled her eyes and I continued with my conversation. "Anyway, we have a lot of time off this weekend for Thanksgiving so could we come over?"

"That's fine with me. Ask Lo and I'll come get y'all." We did and Grandma allowed us to go stay the weekend with our mom. When I we got there, I just stared at her. She was just so beautiful and fly. Like always, she has her gold layered necklaces on, gold bracelets, and diamond rings and earrings to compliment. It was all real too; 24 karat gold. She wasn't into the costume jewelry and all that. She would always see me admiring her jewelry so one time when we took a trip to Atlanta, and she let me wear one of her chains. That was everything to me. I couldn't wait until I got older so I could be fly just like her. However, with my mom, I didn't have to wait. She made sure me, and my two sisters looked just like dolls every time we were with her. That time was no different. She had taken us to the fair, so she dressed her and Ny alike and she dressed me and my baby sister, Toto, alike. People complimented how pretty we were and how nice we were dressed the entire time we were at the fair. It was one of the best weekends I had. After the weekend, we returned home with so many new clothes, shoes, underwear, undershirts, socks, accessories, and toys. You name it, we got it. My mother was away a lot due to incarceration but when she was home or we went with her, she always made sure we had lots of new stuff to keep us looking fresh. It was like that with my mom though. In my eyes, she was that girl. We didn't live with her but the time we spent with her was special.

Christmas time wasn't my favorite time of the year because we didn't have big Christmas' at home, but I loved going to Aunt T.C., my mom's sister, house. She always had a beautiful Christmas display; from her décor, to her tree, to her presents. There were always presents for us and we left with big bags.

CHAPTER THREE

The following school year, I began settling into the school and came to the realization that the more I hated it, the worse it would be. I still had to attend school there so I may as well have gotten comfortable. Plus, I met my friend, Telisha. She was one of the few people I genuinely connected with at school. Our connection was authentic and reciprocal. I cherished that. It was never any animosity, jealousy, or anything like that between us. Telisha was a tomboy, so I always joke that our friendship mirrors the relationship of the sisters on Love and Basketball. As, I am very feminine and was always trying to get her to dress girly or get a cute style done to her hair when she would come over or I would go over her house. I even tried to get her to talk to boys. It was this one boy who was the school, he was in the sixth grade, and he was so fine. He was so smart, and everybody loved him. He was the school president. I tried to get her to talk to him, but she was not having it. All I could do was laugh at her. She was funny and always had a joke up her sleeve.

We really bonded after I discovered how talented I was when it came to basketball. Telisha was already into basketball so one day when Telisha & I were on the basketball court, she passed me the ball. That day we learned I could dribble and shoot. Without ever playing basketball or ever being taught, I was just naturally good. We decided to sign up for our school's basketball team together. Listen – when it came to basketball, we were unstoppable. We were a dynamic duo on the court, and no one could fade us. One time at a game the coach was motioning for me to get in the game but accidentally back handed me and bust my nose wide open. The game has to be paused while I was rushed to the bathroom to clean up the blood. Eventually my nose stopped bleeding. That was cool but I was still upset that my jersey and brand new Jordans had blood on them. Uncle Dirt had just bought me those. He had been buying me fresh sneakers every month since I had started playing basketball at school.

I thought I was going to have a chance to score at least 15 points in them but my coached was benched after I came back from the bathroom for precautionary purposes. They didn't want to be liable if anything happened to me. I was pissed and Telisha was too. When the game resumed, the coach called Telisha to put her in the game, but she refused to play because I couldn't. Our coach was furious that both of her star players were out the game because we were playing our biggest school rivals. We didn't care. Loyalty is royalty where we come from. Our bond was solidified and that's been my dog ever since.

It was this other girl from school named Lay, that I was cool with. I don't really know if I would have considered her a friend because me and her didn't get along all the time. Sometimes we fussed and bickered about stupid stuff, but we kept being phony and still playing with each other like most kids. She was messy though and I hated it because she usually messed with kids that had not done anything to her and to me, that's weak. One day she came over and was knocking on my door but while waiting for a response, she was in hallway being loud. The staff at the housing development that we lived in always complained about us in the hallways so much that they made an offense that can cause a lease termination. I snatched the door open because she definitely wasn't going to be the cause of us losing our home.

"Don't come knocking on my door with all that nonsense going on. Take that where you live at!"

"Who are you talking to Sharda?"

"Who?" I asked puzzled because my intended party was clear. "Who else is banging on the door making all that damn noise in my hallway?" She stepped towards me, and I stepped into the building's hallway closing my house door behind me. Aliyah, another girl from the neighborhood, stuck her hand out between us.

"Okay, okay. I can sense the tension. Whoever thinks they're the baddest one, hit my hand." Aliyah said. We both hit her hand at the same time. Anticipating a fight, I prepared myself because I was just tired of her messing with people. "Y'all did it at the same time. Do it again." We did it again at the same time. "Alright. One last time." By this time, I was over it. So, I just slapped Lay. Everybody grew quiet.

"Did you just slap me?" Lay asked.

"I'll slap your ass again." I said and smiled. I used to go beside our building and practice cussing because where I'm from, when you were a kid and knew how to cuss, arguments just hit different. I had it down pack too because I could cuss you out so bad you would cry to your mother. I had actually never been in a fight before then and wasn't anxious about fighting Layla. I wasn't scared at all. She was a little bigger than me but that was fine. My mother taught me *The bigger they are, the harder they fall.* I slapped her again and we fought. I was impressed at myself at how good I could fight being this was my first real fight. I didn't even notice that I had slammed Lay on the ground, and I was stomping her so hard. "Bitch. . . Bitch. . . Bitch . . .!" I screamed with each kick.

"Hey! Hey! Hey! Y'all stop!" Grandma yelled pulling me off of Lay. "I didn't know what the hell all that damn noise was going on out here. Get your ass in the house. Out here fighting with these fake ass kids." That was my way out. I vowed then that I was never going to let anyone bully me again. That's when I realized I could fight really good like my mom.

When we went back to school the following Monday, the teacher asked Lay had she been run over by a truck. She said that she was in a fight with me. Then at lunch, everybody was coming up to me in the cafeteria asking about the fight; making jokes and mocking fighting stances and they weren't even there. Mind you, these are the same mean, rude kids that had been going to the school. Only difference was, they knew not to play with me now. Everyone talked about that fight for a while; especially family and friends in my neighborhood. I remember hearing Grandma was on the phone with one of her friends bragging about how I beat Lay down.

"Yeah girl. Sharda beat her ass. I bet they'll leave her alone now." She laughed.

CHAPTER FOUR

Fifth grade year started off a lot better. After beating Lay's ass, it was my guess that my other school mates realized that I wasn't the one to be fucked with. That was cool with me because I wanted to focus on my keeping my grades up so I could keep playing basketball. However, I'm sure you know that it's always that one person that has to try you. One day we were outside for recess playing kickball and for the first time, I was enjoying myself. Everyone was getting along, laughing, running around, and just having fun.

"Let me see what you got!" My classmate Renee called out and we giggled as it was my turn to kick.

"Okay, I'm going to show you what I got." I said confidently. Drawing my foot back while simultaneously throwing the ball up, I aligned it perfectly. When I did kick the ball, it went over the kids heads that I was playing with and hit Brittany Parker dead smack in the face. Brittany was one of the most popular girls in the entire school, so the reactions were mixed. Some people laughed and others stared anxiously as she glared at me.

"Oh my God! Are you okay? I apologize." I started sincerely.

"I don't want no fucking apologies. Watch where you kick that ball or I'm going to kick your ass.

"I didn't do it on purpose but I'm not apologizing again." I responded and walked off. Recess was over and all of the classes were headed back inside the school. With my teacher's permission, I went to the restroom before returning to class. As soon as I entered, I noticed Brittany and her friends. It didn't bother me though, so I proceeded to an empty stall. Once I was finished and came out, I was washing my hands as I noticed Brittany coming towards me.

"What's all that stuff you were talking outside?" She snarled.

"What?" I asked with a look of confusion because I did not understand how this girl could have misinterpreted what I said. My first and only apology was all that I was issuing out because I wasn't kissing nobody's ass. "Excuse me." I disregarded her presence and I attempted to walk pass her and she smacked me. My body tensed to the point that I felt hot. I froze. Fear was not an emotion I experienced as I wasn't scared at all. Her palms were always sweaty and clammy, and her nails were dirty and claw-like. Disgust filled me. I really didn't want her touching me. One time she beat this boy up and he had so many scratches all over his face. Before I could react, my teacher opened the restroom door.

"Is there a problem in here, Dominica?" She asked as if she could sense the tension in the air. I didn't respond immediately as I continued to glare at Brittany. "Dominica. . ." My teacher called out again breaking me from my thoughts.

"No ma'am. It's no problem." Walking out of the bathroom, I smiled at Brittany and made a mental that I was going to beat her ass. Maybe not today but for sure, she had an ass whipping coming from me. Once I got back to class, I was angry and couldn't focus. I wanted to fight so bad that I couldn't pay attention to what my teacher was saying. All I thought about was getting my revenge. Once I got home from school, I still didn't even play because I was thinking about how I would get her back. The next day when I went to school, I hoped that I would catch in the bathroom again.

While sitting in class goofing off with some friends, the school's guidance counselor, Ms. Lavell, came and got me and walked me to the office. The only thing I could of is that I was in some type of trouble. However, when I arrived, Ny was already in the office. I didn't know what was wrong, but I knew it was something. Ms. Lavell invited us into the main office's conference room. I sat down in one of the comfortable rotating chairs and began spinning around.

"What's going on?" Ny asked but Ms. Lavell didn't respond immediately.

"I'm sorry to have to tell y'all this here but I thought it would be best if you heard it together." Ms. Lavell started. "We received a call that your mom that has passed away." Life paused for a few seconds as I tried to consume what I had just heard. Tears uncontrollably escaped both of our eyes. "I'm so sorry that you both have to go through this. We are here for you so please don't hesitate to utilize us a resource. Your grandmother has been notified and she's on her way to get you." Shortly after, we could hear Grandma cussing all the way down the hallway.

"I don't give a damn! Where is these kids at? Where is these kids at?" We ran to her immediately. "Come on y'all. Everything is going to be okay. Let's just go home." Grandma comforted us.

CHAPTER FIVE

The next day, grandma didn't even wake us up for school. It was silent in our home outside of Grandma making a few calls trying to figure out what was going on. Grandma ended up taking us to Grandma Hattie's house later that day. You would have thought that our mom was a celebrity because it was so many people there to mourn her passing and pay their respects to our family. Everyone sat around drinking, laughing, crying, and sharing their fondest memories of my mom. Me, Ny, and Toto sat together in silence, comforting one another. The house phone rung and my Aunt Tracy answered.

"Girl, you got everybody over here crying and shit!" Aunt Tracy said into phone. "Tonya ass ain't dead. She's on the phone y'all." My mom had been incarcerated. We talked to her for a while. I told my mom what had happened with Brittany slapping me in the bathroom and she was livid. She told me then, *Dominica Sims, I don't give a fuck what the consequences are, you better not ever let a mother fucker play with you like that again.* My mom could fight really good, so she didn't play that shit. Everyone was so relieved and took turns cussing my mom out for the scare and expressing their joy that she was still alive.

The summer before Middle School went pass pretty fast but it was so much fun. Now, it was time for middle school. South Middle School was my assigned school but not Telisha's, so we were both sad that we weren't going to the same school. However, guess what? Our schools were sports rivals because we were both good teams, so we got to play against one another which made the games even more interesting, and we definitely packed the gyms out on game nights. It was still weird not seeing her a lot since we were used to seeing each other daily. We started to develop our lives with new friends in our new schools.

Well, I socialized with many people, but I only had one friend, Tiffany. We met over the summer and realized had a lot in common as we were both into fashion, boys, and we both could fight well. She became a really good friend of mine, so we spent a lot of time together. So much time that her little sisters used to accuse her of acting funny when I came over. It wasn't that; we just vibed. We found solace in each other's realness. You know *real is rare*.

At my new school, South Middle School, it was cool and laid back. Of course, there were fights and arguments like any other school, but everybody did their own thing and didn't just bother with people intentionally. That was just the culture of the school, which was good because I damn sure wasn't the same girl that Brittany had slapped in the bathroom years before, but I was more into dressing cute and kicking it with my friends. However, you know when your reputation exceeds you, it's always going to be at least one person that tries you.

One day in the beginning of the school year on an early Monday morning, I had a fight with a girl about the last seat in the back of the bus. You know everyone wants to sit in the last seat. The school bus pulled up while I was checking my attire, so I closed my pocket mirror and boarded the bus. People stared at me as I made my way to the back of the bus and took the last seat. It didn't bother me as I figured it was because I was new, pretty, and fly. I would stare too. I took out my pocket mirror and applied a tad bit of lip gloss as I admired myself. At the next stop, a girl got on the bus and everybody's eyes followed her as she walked towards me.

"Get out of my seat!" She demanded. I sized her up and look back down in my pocket mirror.

"If you don't sit your silly ass down somewhere." I spat.

"I am. Right there in my seat." She said and stepped a bit closer.

"Come sit with me Trish." A girl called out to her from a few rows up.

"Yeah, go on up there because I'm not moving." I giggled a little as she walked away. She turned around before she took her seat and looked at me.

"If you're in my seat when we get out of school, I'm going to beat your ass. Watch."

"See you then." I responded as I snapped my mirror closed and crossed my legs. She had a rude awakening coming if she thought she was going to whip my ass. I went on about my day as normal; going to class, joking around and talking to Tiffany and other school mates, and playing basketball in Gym class. I couldn't wait for the bell to ring. After school, I ran to the bus so I could make sure I was sitting in the last seat. When she got on the bus, she was hype as hell with her crew. That didn't faze me at all. She looked at me and rolled her eyes and I chuckled while shaking my head in disgust. It irritated me when somebody's talked a bunch of shit and then when it came time to fight, they punked out. Not with me though. She was going to have to back that shit up she was talking. She was going to have to show me. When the bus came to my stop, I remained seated.

"Let's go young lady." The bus driver shouted, exposing that he had caught on to my plan to get off at her stop. I grabbed my bookbag and proceeded to get off the bus. As soon as I stepped off the front of the bus, I heard her call out to me.

"We going to see tomorrow bitch!" She yelled as the bus driver closed the bus doors fast. I banged the bus door as he pulled off. I geeked up all the kids that got off at my bus stop; including Lil Lord and Nunu to run down to her bus stop with me.

"I'm going to beat her ass." I said as we ran. When she got off the bus, I beat her ass for running her mouth and making me run.

"Cuz, you beat her ass!" Lil Lord said after the first.

"I ain't playing with these bitches this year!" I responded as he put his arm on my shoulder and we walked back down Florence towards Woodberry. Needless to say, I never had a problem out of her anymore and I sat wherever I chose to comfortably every day on that bus.

I didn't really get into too much after that. Primarily because I didn't lose sight of my goals in school or sports. Even though I wasn't going to allow people to play with me, I was determined not to allow fighting to consume my energy. Instead, basketball continued to be my outlet and I let it have my focus which resulted in me leading my school to the championship game. Everyone was excited too. The bleachers were filled with parents and students from both schools. I waved at Grandma, Aunt Meka, and Ny in the bleachers because the game started. They smiled and waved back. Though we were in the lead, I had only scored 4 points in the first quarter, and I wasn't feeling that. My coach must could tell.

"Sims, you got this!" He shouted to me. I nodded my head in agreement before closing my eyes and stretching. When second quarter started, I was back in my groove, I shouted two 3 pointers. After my second one, I heard a familiar voice yelling from the bleachers.

"Yeahhhh! That's my baby right there! Stop playing with her! Get 'em Sharda!" A familiar voice screamed. I looked up towards the voice to see my mom's face. I thought I was tripping, but when I realized that I wasn't, my smile spread so wide that my cheeks started to turn red. Her energy and my desire to show her how great I was at basketball made me turn it up a notch. I scored 28 points that game and it was one of the best games I played in my middle school years. The best part was that my mom was there to witness it. She had actually come home the same day and came straight to my game. I expressed my gratitude, but I am still not sure she knows how much that meant to me.

CHAPTER SIX

"What are you thinking about girl?" Tiffany asked snapping me from my thoughts.

"Girlllll! All types of stuff. I don't know why but it just be popping up in my mind!" I said and we both laughed.

"I can tell because I'm asking you if my outfit is cute or too much and you were zoned out." We were getting ready so that we could go skating with the Teen Center. The Teen Center was a place where all of the kids in the neighborhood could go and hang out, chill, socialize, play games, and go on trips. It was always free or low cost too. I thought that was cool because most parents were struggling to make ends meet but their kids were still afforded the opportunity to enjoy different fun activities that they might have not been able to afford without the center.

"My bad girl. You look bomb though. You knew that! You just wanted me to say it!" I responded, playfully rolling my eyes.

"You already know. It's different from someone else's view. Who better than you? At least I know you're going to keep it real with me." Tiffany said.

"That's true. You look fly as usual."

"I know." She said and we chuckled about that too. It was always a good time with us. Similar to my friendship with Telisha, it was no catty competition or phoniness.

The skating rink we were going to was Roller World and I was excited. I love it there. My godmother, whose name was also Tiffany, used to pick me and take me places, including Roller World for years. Eventually, she had her own baby, so she didn't have as much time as she used to. We remained in contact though and she was still always there for me. We made sure we were looking bomb because going to Roller World was equivalent to adults going to the club. You never knew who you were going to see because it was teen night and teens from all over the city came. We both knew a lot of people so when we went, we socialized the entire night. Afterwards, while we waited for the van to pick us up, you would not believe who my eyes landed on. Brittany Parker! Yup, the sweaty, clammy handed girl that smacked me in the bathroom in first grade. I did not care how many years ago it was. There is no statute of limitation on revenge. I took off my jewelry and tucked it securely in my pocket. Noticing my mood shift and actions, Tiffany began to take her jewelry off as well.

"Naw. I got this." I said to Tiffany.

"Okay and I got you. What are you talking about?" Tiffany screwed her face up, disregarded my statement, and proceeded to take her jewelry off. She followed me as I approached Brittany. Tapping on Brittany's shoulder, she turned around and I cocked my hand back and slapped her as hard as I could before beating her up. I got straight to it. There was nothing to talk about. I never break a promise; especially not to myself. There was no need for Tiffany to jump in because I whipped Brittany's ass really good. I was still beating her up when the van arrived, so Tiffany pulled me off of her as all the kids ran to the van.

"You slapped the wrong bitch!" I screamed and held up both of my middle finger as I jogged backwards a little before turning around to run to the van.

"Yeah! Stop playing with my friend!" Tiffany hyped me after we flopped down in our seats on the van. "You really whipped her ass!" We laughed.

"I owed that bitch that ass whipping. That's the same girl that slapped me in the fifth grade."

"Girlllll! She ain't never gonna slap another bitch." Tiffany said matter-of-factly.

"Ever!" I said as we high-fived.

When I walked in the house from the skating rink, there was a boy sitting there. I was confused because he looked like my cousins and my Uncle Dirt.

"Chi, this your cousin Randy, my son. Randy, this is your cousin Sharda, but I call her Chi. She's your Uncle Dominic's daughter." Uncle Dirt said introducing us. Randy and I sat on Grandma's back porch talking and we realized that we had a lot in common. Not only were we the same age, but we both played basketball. From this day forward. Randy and were locked in like brother and sister.

CHAPTER SEVEN

My cousins Ayanna and Neshia always came up for the summer time and stayed at Grandma's house. In the middle of the summer, we ended up moving away to our new house in a predominantly white neighborhood. Though I was sad about moving, our summer was non-stop fun and went a lot of places. One day while we were all jumping on the bed, Grandma warned us to stop

"Y'all better stop jumping on that bed!" Ten minutes later, we started jumping again and Ayanna fell and cut her leg open. Thankfully the was the worst thing that happened during the summer. The summer ended quickly it seemed and Ayanna and Neshia had to go home. We were all sad, but we already looked forward to next summer.

My new school, Portage Central Middle School, probably the worse of them all because not only were the students mean and racist, but most of the teachers were also. Basketball still had my interest, and my skills were better than ever. I practiced all summer because at our new house, we had a basketball hoop in our driveway. At basketball tryouts, I performed at my highest potential and worked really hard to show the coach what I had. The Portage Central girls were trash and didn't take practice seriously.

"Basketball is about playing as a team. Showing off is not good sportsmanship." The coach yelled to me after practice. *What the fuck were you watching sir? What the hell do you think I was doing?* I thought to myself because that's exactly why I pulled back on my game so that I could see how we worked as a team. There were so many turnovers in practice because they couldn't even catch. The following Monday, everyone was checking roster, but I waited patiently because I already knew I made the team. Sadly, I was mistaken. Immediately, I went to the gym to see the coach.

"Coach Barnes, I'm confused. So, I didn't make the team because I'm good?" I asked confused.

"No, you didn't make the team because you didn't get an athletic physical."

"I have my physical scheduled for Thursday. That's already in order."

"Thursday is too late. Physicals were due yesterday." He responded and walked off. Of course, I knew that an athletic physical was a requirement to participate in basketball, but not once did he ever mention that it was a requirement to be chosen for the team. My disgust for the school grew instantly. When I returned to class, I felt defeated. I made up a story about not feeling well so that I could be sent home early. Grandma came to pick me up.

"Have you talked to Ny?" She asked me once I got in the car. "She still hasn't come home."

"Yes, she said she was going to her friend's house when she left the other day." I responded. Two days prior, I walked in on Ny packing a bag and when I asked her where she was going, she responded to her friend's house. Thinking about it now, I realized she did pack a lot of clothes to just be staying the night at a friend's. I hoped she'd come home soon though because I missed her, and it was lonely without her. As if she could feel me missing her, she called a few days later. The weekend was coming up and I asked Grandma if I could go stay the weekend with Mary at Aunt Bell's house. While I was there, I talked to them about how the coach had treated me and feeling defeated. Ultimately, Grandma and Aunt Bell agreed that I could stay with Aunt Bell so that I could go back to South Middle.

CHAPTER EIGHT

Staying with Aunt Bell was fun; especially since Mary and I got to be together every day. School was going well too, and I was back on the court playing basketball with my old team. One day after practice, I was walking to the bus stop with my teammates when some girls starting walking behind us, nitpicking. As bad as I wanted to fight, I wanted to stay on the team more. Coach had already let us know that any conflict, inside or outside of school would lead to us being put off the team. Basketball was the good thing in my life and my outlet. When all else failed I could rely on it to make me feel good. Were the girls easy to avoid? No. But the choice not to fall for their trap was necessary.

When I walked in the house, Aunt Bell was sitting in the living room.

"Hey Sharda. You need to call this number and check on your mom. She's in the hospital." She said and handed me a slip of paper containing the number. I called the number several times but got no answer. I decided to lay back down until Mary got home. Once she did, she sat on the bed with and rubbed her fingers through my hair as I cried. She knew that I was worried about my mom, so she listened as I reminisced about her. We laughed and cried and laughed some more. In the middle of me acting out a story I was sharing about a time that my mom was fighting the police, the phone rang.

"Hello." I answered the phone.

"Sharda. . ." My mom said weakly.

"Ma!" I said as Mary and I looked at each other, relieved. I talked to my mom for a few and when I hung up, I said to Mary, "I have to go see my mom." We jumped up to put our coats on and caught the city bus to the hospital

My mom had been shot several times in her legs. Seeing my mother laid up in that hospital bed with her legs wrapped up really hurt my heart. My Mom explained what happened to her and how they left her for dead. I was so sad at how cruel the world could be. My Mom said as she laid on the ground asking for help, two people stepped right over her. I washed her up, combed her hair, and got her dinner set up for her. My mom had such a great sense of humor. She explained to us that the doctor said she'd never be able to walk again. I sat there in tears as I couldn't hold them back anymore.

"Mom, don't worry. I can just move in with you and help you." I offered.

"Yeah, Tonya, I don't mind helping you too." Mary said as she cried.

"I love y'all and I appreciate y'all." My mom responded. We sat there for a long time. So long that we hid when visiting hours were over and came back out after they checked the rooms. I made my mom promise to call me every day while she was in the hospital. The buses had stopped running by the time we were ready to leave and neither of us had any money. We hadn't considered any of that before leaving. I just knew that I had to see my mom and hug her. I didn't want to worry her with how I was getting home. I just wanted her to rest and get better so she could be discharged. As we left, I said a silent prayer in my head for her.

"Aye, I have an idea." Mary said as we entered the lobby of the hospital. "Follow me!" She said as she pulled my arm. Mary and I got into one of the cabs in front of the hospital. She instructed me that she was going to tell the driver we had two stops. The first stop was an address near the split by Aunt Bell's house. She would get out at the split and go inside the building. After she entered, I was to count to 60 and then act like I was irritated and was coming to get her. As soon as I entered the building, we ran out the opposite door and across the lot to Aunt Bell's house. As soon as we got inside, we collapsed into the chair breathless. We could see a pair of head lights flash through the window and keep going. I peeked out the window and saw it was the cab. The driver was circling the block. I collapsed back into the chair. We laughed about that all night before falling asleep.

Months passed and my mom had doing so much better since being discharged from the hospital. Despite what the doctors had predicted for her, she was even walking again. We talked on the phone every day and I was just so happy that God answered my prayers for her. Mary had gotten her own apartment a few doors down from Aunt Bell with her boyfriend, Cruz. I had graduated 8th grade and had moved on to high school, but I was still going to school on their side of town, so I stayed between the Aunt Bell and Mary's houses. High school was a different world for me. I fought so much more, and I was better at it. It didn't make matters any better that a lot of my cousins went to school with me.

Though I had my fair share of trouble in school, I didn't lose sight of my athletic aspirations. It was basketball tryouts, ninth grade year. The coach was impressed to say the least. I was too excited. The only issue was that our dues were $400 and due up front. It wasn't even a whole week before it was due, and I had no idea who to ask for it. Grandma didn't have it and I didn't feel right asking her anyway, she was already stretched thin. Still, I tried my luck, but she confirmed what I already knew – that she couldn't afford to give me that kind of money at the time. My second call was to my father. His car wash seemed to be doing well. Besides, you would think that he would want to help me as I had worked at the car wash plenty of times with my cousin, Randy – with no pay may I add.

"Hello?" My father answered the phone, and I took a deep breath.

"Hey. How are you?"

"Shiddddd. I'm doing well. I can't complain at all. What's up Sharda?"

"Well. . ." I started.

"Well, what? What you got in some trouble?"

"Not at all. Actually, I've been doing good. I need $400 for my basketball dues."

"Four hundred dollars? Damn! Why are they so high? I don't have no $400. You asked Lo? What did she say?"

"Yes, I have. She doesn't have it."

"What about Tonya? Call her and see what she says. I'll come up with a couple dollars for you."

"Thanks Dad. I'll let you know what she says." I was sad but not disappointed because at least he offered to try to come up with something. Being as though my mom was still recovering, I initially opted to not call her. Feeling defeated, I laid back down and looked at the ceiling. *What the hell? It couldn't hurt to try though, right?* I though picked up the phone and called her.

"Hello?" She answered the phone in a sweet tone.

"Hey Ma. Its Sharda."

"Heyyy baby girl! What's going on?" She said in a bubbly tone, instantly putting me in a better mood.

"Ma, I need $400 for my basketball dues, and I've already asked everyone. They are all saying they don't have it. I know that's a lot and you may not have it either but. . ."

"When is it due?" She asked cutting my rant off.

"Tomorrow at practice."

"Damn. Okay."

"Yeah, I know so if you don't have it, I understand. I know it's a lot and its due so soon."

"What time is the practice over?" She asked ignoring my attempts to expect the worst.

"Five o'clock."

"Let me see what I can do." She said.

"Yes ma'am." It was a good feeling that she cared enough to try but, I wasn't optimistic about the outcome though. We talked and laughed some more before hanging up, I actually left the conversation feeling a lot better than I did when I first called. My mother's personality was like that though. It was positive, fun, and contagious. Morning came fast. Where I usually was very upbeat and ready for the day, I dragged that day. I packed my backpack with my books and my basketball practice attire and made my way to school.

The school day went surprisingly fast. I contemplated not going to basketball practice, but I decided to go ultimately. I figured I'd ask the coach for an extension on my dues so I could come up with the money. However, I lost the courage to do so. Instead, I decided to act like I was sick all practice. Thirty minutes into practice, the coach benched me because I was playing lousy. That was more so due to me feeling defeated, than acting sick.

"Alright, there are few people that still need to pay dues. You know who you are. See me after practice. Today is the deadline. Failure to pay your dues today will result in you not being able to play. You will be able to practice but you will get no game time. No exceptions." Silent tears found their way down my face as I slid down in my seat at the top of the bleachers. After looking at my watch, I put my face in my shirt. It was 4:45pm and I hadn't worked up the nerve to ask coach for an extension. After his announcement, I didn't think I was going to either. I got up and started to make my way down the bleachers and the gym doors opened. I couldn't believe my eyes. My mother sashayed in looking like a fashion model. I ran down the bleachers to her and gave her a hug. "Someone's feeling better I see." My coach said and walked over to us. "May I help you ma'am?"

"Are you the coach?" My mom asked Coach.

"I am." Coach responded.

"My name is Tanya. I'm Dominica's mother."

"Your daughter is a natural star."

"Trust me. I know. I only birth excellence. I came to pay her dues." My mom said handing Coach an envelope full of cash.

"Thank you. I'm not sure if you saw the flyer but her dues include game uniforms, practice uniforms, and transportation to away games."

"Fair enough. As long as my baby can do what makes her happy." She said and looked at me smiling. Grabbing my things from the locker room and changing, I hurried so that I could leave with my mom.

"You're going to be feeling better next week, right Dominica?" Coach asked in a knowing tone.

"Yes, I am." I responded. I was so excited. Little did he know. I was feeling better already.

"Good, I need all my star players on their A game."

The following week when I returned to school, everyone bragged about how pretty and fly my mother was and how much we looked alike. That was nothing new to me, everywhere we went, everyone always complimented my mother and her girls because our physical appearance was always on point. I was admiring my mother for different reasons. She done things for me in the past but, her coming through for me with my basketball dues in less than 24 hours gave me a new level of respect for her. It solidified that no matter what anyone said about my mother, she would do anything in her power for us. That made my love for her grow founder.

CHAPTER NINE

Lately, I had been staying at Mary's apartment more than Aunt Bell's. So much that I wasn't even going home to Grandma's house on the weekends like I used to. This weekend was no different in that regard. However, Mary and her boyfriend did have company over that weekend – her boyfriend's cousin, Shawn, and his baby mother, Myesha, from Chicago. My plan was to chill with them in the day time and sleep at Aunt Bell's at night so that their guest would have a place to sleep.

The music was jamming and the vibes were chill as everyone was enjoying themselves. I was used to being around Mary and Cruz all the time, but Shawn and Myesha were both really cool too – at first. Shortly after he started drinking, I felt Shawn looking at me a couple times but every time I looked at him, he'd look away. That was cool with me because I wasn't interested. Besides, his baby mother was right there. Niggas had no regard to their disrespect. After a few hours of drinking, Shawn was wasted and was not at all discreet about his intentions as he openly begun to flirt with me. While in the kitchen getting some juice, I leaned in the refrigerator to pour my cup so I didn't hear Shawn enter the kitchen.

"Damn, I know that pussy tight and wet." He said startling me. I jumped up, almost dropping my cup of juice. "Why you so jumpy?" He asked and brushed my hair back out my face.

"Nigga, I didn't hear you in here. Why wouldn't I be jumpy? You startled me."

"Damn you are so sexy to me." He said to me with lust in his eyes.

"Sexy to you? I'm 14 and you're what? 21? 22?" I asked, rolling my eyes.

"What does age have to do with it?"

"Everything. What do you mean?" I said clearly getting irritated. Everyone else was still into the music and partying and seemingly hadn't noticed that he wasn't in there with them. He went back into the living room, and I went to the bathroom. As I was washing my hands, there was a knock at the bathroom door. It was Shawn. I opened the door and he stood in the doorway smiling.

"Why are you so fucking pretty?" He asked, obviously well pass the limit his drinking tolerance could handle.

"I don't know. Ask God or my parents." I retorted. "Get out of my way though."

"I want to feel that pussy." He slurred.

"No!"

"Come on pretty. I'll be gentle." He begged.

"NO! What part of that don't you understand?"

"Let me just eat it then." He pleaded.

"NO!" I said pushing pass him.

We all were sitting in the living room for a while listening to R. Kelly's TP2. I felt myself getting tired, so I went and got my stuff ready to get in the shower. After I got out of shower, Shawn came into the bathroom. I attempted to leave out.

"Move!" I said but he didn't move.

"Let me taste you." He said with a devilish grin.

"No. Move." I said and tried to push him out the way of the door, but he did move. In fact, he pinned me to the wall, pulled the towel up, and proceeded to give me head. He had no regard for my attempts to push him off of me. His strength was unmatched as I was unsuccessful in fighting him off me. When he finished, he released his grip and proceeded to use the bathroom as if he didn't just violate me. I pulled my and ran out of the bathroom. As I walked through the living room, I noticed that Myesha was passed out drunk and Mary and Cruz were no longer in the living room. I left and went next door to Aunt Bell's and jumped in the shower again immediately. I sat down in the shower and let the water run all over me as I put my head down in between my legs.

After my shower, I called Grandma and asked if I could move back home, and she agreed. No one asked any questions or was even concerned about why I abruptly decided to leave and come back home. Since being home, I spent a lot of time with my nephew, Donnie, Ny's son that she conceived when she ran away. Donnie and I were really close.

One day, I was listening to music and cleaning up with my cousin, Tiesha, Uncle Terry's daughter who had come to stay with us for a while and Lil. Wayne's Hot Girl came on.

"I like 'em hot! The ones that don't tell me to stop. . ." I quoted the lyrics word for word as Lil Wayne was my favorite rapper, so I knew all of his lyrics verbatim. "I need a project bitch, a hood rat bitch, one that don't a damn and say she took that shit!" Unbeknownst to me, Uncle Terry was standing right behind me. He grabbed me by my neck, digging his nails in my skin, and slammed me to the ground. Blood was dripping down my neck.

"You too young! Y'all too grown! Shouldn't even be listening to this music!" He yelled. Uncle Terry had come home from prison and was tethered to Grandma's house. The next day, I left the phone off the hook and unplugged his tether box so that his parole officer could come to the house and violate him. He wasn't about to keep putting his hands on us. He wasn't our Daddy. Two hours after I unplugged it, there was a knock at the door. I ran to the door and swung it open. Six police officers and a white stood at our door.

"Yup, he's in here! Come right on in." I said before they could even get a chance to say anything. They came in and got Uncle Terry and told him that he had violated his parole by tampering with his tether box.

"That boy been here all day. Ain't nobody mess with that damn tether! One of them damn kids had to do it!" Grandma yelled, but despite her pleas, they still arrested him. Grandma looked behind the table to see that the tether box was unplugged and when she paged the phone, it beeped under my pillow. She was so mad at me and very overwhelmed. She started yelling.

"I'm sick of your raggedy ass. I'm boutta look for me a one-bedroom apartment or senior citizen apartment where no kids can be." Keeping her word, Grandma decided to move into a retirement home. Eventually, Ny had come back home, so her, Donnie and I moved in with Aunt Meka. While living with Aunt Meka, we saw Toto more often because she visited us and eventually moved in with us. We were so happy that we were all together. We all did each other's hair and made sure that we all had clean clothes. We shared everything and made sure each other didn't go without. One day while sitting on the porch, Toto told me that she saw our mom, and that mom gave her $50. Mom told her to let us know that she loved us and gave us a number where we could contact her.

"I might go back to Grandma Hattie's." Toto said.

"If you go back to Grandma Hattie's house, I'm going with you." I responded. In that conversation, Toto expressed her feelings about missing Grandma Hattie. I understood because I missed Grandma as well.

The next day, while driving pass the projects, we saw Driver and Big D's bodies lying on the ground. This put the whole hood in an uproar. We couldn't believe somebody had executed them. Although I didn't really know Big D, I had a very close relationship with Driver so this saddened me.

Eventually, we ended up moving in with Grandma Hattie. The conditions weren't ideal, but I was happy to be there with my sisters. The main issue was that Grandma Hattie had roaches. One day while I was in class, a roach came out of my backpack. Immediately, I started to panic.

Quietly, I hurried and stepped on it and looked around to see if anyone had seen it. They hadn't but I was still embarrassed.

After school, I was in a much better mood because I was chilling with my cousin Mack. He was a big-time hustler so of course everyone was in awe when he picked me up from school in his foreign car. We stopped so that I could get some food and I ate in the car while he drove around and handled his business. As he drove me to Tiffany's house, we talked about school, basketball, and just life in general. Mack had always genuinely been there for me and never neglected to give me real advice.

"Never trust anyone but God and yourself." He said and looked at me seriously. "Do you hear me? Never trust anyone but God and you, Sharda. Real shit." Just as I was about to respond, I noticed Tiffany arguing with a group of girls.

"Pull over!" I demanded Mack. Before the car could make a full stop, I hopped out.

"What's the problem?" I asked as I approached the group.

"What bitch?" An ugly girl asked as she stepped forward. Tiffany and I looked at each other and that was it. We started fucking them up; one by one. I had enough anger in me to beat a football team that day. Tiffany must have felt the same. We whipped their asses – just the two of us – and carried on with our evening as usual.

Once I got home to Grandma Hattie's house, I went upstairs to lay down. I looked at the clock and it was 10:10pm. Shortly after closing my eyes, I heard the noise of someone coming in, but I pretended that I was sleep. It was a woman because I could hear her heels clacking as she walked up the stairs. The woman entered the room and took a seat in the chair that sat in the corner of the room. I peeked and realized it was my mom and she was wearing this pretty red dress. I didn't say anything. I just smiled and closed my eyes again. The sound of her shuffling things in her purse caused me to curiously peek and see what she was looking for. When I reopened my eyes, a big cloud of grey smoke loomed around her and in her hand appeared to be a glass bottle.

CHAPTER TEN

Some time had passed, and it had been a while since I had seen my mother. I wasn't feeling it, so I went to look for her. It would make me feel better to know that she was okay. After visiting some of her frequently visited places, I ended up in front of a house Ada Ave. Now, I wasn't surprised that I couldn't find my mom because often times when she's in the streets, she'd isolate from her family. She didn't want people to see her like that. I don't care how she was feeling. I just wanted to see her. *You always trying to run up behind her raggedy ass. You're going to end up just like her in jail somewhere.* Grandma's voice haunted my thoughts as I stood on the sidewalk, looking up at the house. I didn't care what she was or what she did. None of that trumped her being my mother and I was going to love her for her regardless. Two guys came out of the front door of the house.

"Hey. Is my mom in there?" I asked them.

"Who?" The older of the two guys asked.

"Tonya. She's about. . ." I started.

"No! Get away from here. This is no place for a kid. If I see her, I'll let her know you're looking for her. But she's not in there." He said cutting me off. He was so fucking rude.

"Yes, she is." The younger guy said. "She upstairs. Second bedroom." If looks could kill, the older man would be wanted for murder. His eyes pierced through the soul of the younger man. They could sort that out. I needed to see my mom, so I walked pass them into the house. The smell as soon as I opened the door almost took my breath. Gasping for air, I coughed repeatedly as I stepped into the living room. That didn't turn me around though. I was determined to find my mother.

"Who the hell is that doing all that damn coughing?" A lady's voice fussed from a back area where I'm guessing the kitchen was. "You are about to get your ass beat disturbing my mother fucking high." She continued as I made my way to the step. "Sharda?" I turned around to see Ms. Betty, my mother's long-time friend. "Get out of here right now! Go!" She shouted sternly and I ran out the front door and down the street. I stopped to catch my breath and breathe in some fresh air. Tears began to pour from my eyes. I coughed and coughed and coughed.

"Sharda! Dominica! Sharda!" Instantly, I recognized my mother's voice calling out to me. I turned around to find her jogging down the street towards me. Once she got to me, she hugged me so tight, and I hugged her back. "Why are you crying? Did anyone hurt you? Who was it? One of them mother fuckers at that house?" She rambled off questions.

"No. No one did anything to me." I assured her as we walked to the Polar Bear so that we could talk. "I was worried about you. I wanted to make sure nothing happened to you."

"I'm okay daughter." She said even though I could look at her and see she wasn't. She was still beautiful but there was a certain darkness in her eyes and her hands were very dark.

"Well, I'm glad you're okay. Do you stay in that house? It stinks!" I said and she laughed a little.

"I just visit my friends there sometimes but, I don't want you to ever come back here for any reason. I promise I will call more so that you are not worried. Just never come back to that house and damn sure don't go inside there." We talked and cried for a long while before I had to go.

"Come home Ma."

"I'm coming." She responded sincerely. We hugged and went our separate ways.

My friend Danisha's mom, Ms. Neen, had gotten me a job at McDonalds so she had been letting me stay at their house most nights that I worked. I didn't have to work tonight but I had asked Ms. Neen if I could stay over anyway, and she agreed. Danisha and her family were always kind to me, and I appreciated it. They knew my living conditions at Grandma Hattie's so they tried their best to help me out as much as they could.

As the weekend approached, everyone prepared for my friend Jay's house party. I had gotten my first check and went to the mall to buy me and Toto a pair of Jordans and matching outfits for us to wear to the party. Everybody from both high schools showed up so Lizzy Street was packed. Everyone was outside because there was no more room in the party. Around Midnight, we walked Toto home and came back. When we returned, the police had shown up and started making everyone move. The crowd was so rowdy that the police even started making people. We sat on the porch until Jay's mom made us come in the house. Jay and I had already planned for me to stay for a few days.

On Sunday evening, I took a shower to wash the day off of me. It had most definitely been a long one recovering from the party. As I left the bathroom, I bumped into Dontay, Jay's older brother.

"Just who I was looking for." He smiled with a devilish grin.

"What the hell were you looking for me for?"

"You're going to give me some of that pussy or I'm going to tell my mother that your homeless ass the one that stole her diamond bracelet." Jay's mom, Pearl, diamond tennis bracelet had been missing for a while. She was under the impression that she had misplaced it.

"What? I would never steal from Pearl! Are you crazy?"

"I know you didn't. I have the bracelet and I have plans for it." He laughed holding up the bracelet. "But who do you think she's going to believe; her son who has never stole anything from her in his life or her daughter's homeless friend who came to stay with us just before her bracelet went missing?" He licked his lips and I glared at him.

Jay and Pearl hadn't made it in yet so there was there was no sense in me yelling or shouting. Besides, I learned a long time ago that no one was coming to save me. I had always had to save myself. Disgust is the only emotion I could use to describe how I felt in that moment. I glanced at the room where I slept and contemplated how I was going to manage this situation because it was no way this boy was touching me. Slowly and seductively, I stepped closer to him. His confidence quickly transformed into desperation as he lusted over me. I almost laughed at his stupidity. *There is always a way to defeat your opponent. Fighting is more than physical. It's mental. Control your opponent's mental and you've already won the battle before you even strike.* I heard my mother's voice in my head clear as day. Without a second thought, I grabbed him by the balls and twisted them. He screamed and crippled over in pain, but I did not loosen my grip.

"Hoe ass nigga, if you ever in your fucking life come near me again, I will cut your dick off myself. Do you understand me?" He grunted but didn't respond. I tightened my grip and yelled, "Do you fucking understand me?"

"Yes! Yes! Yes! I understand. Just let my shit go you crazy bitch!" He cried out and I let go.

"Stay the fuck away from me or you'll really see crazy." I snarled. I went in the room and packed my stuff as tears slowly started to fall from my eyes. Immediately, I went straight back to Grandma Hattie's house.

"What you doing coming in here so late? Thought you went back to Loraine's house." She fussed as she opened the door.

"Just because I haven't been staying here doesn't mean that I don't live here." I snapped but checked myself. "I'll be home a lot more now though."

"What you got on Grandma's beer baby?" Grandma Hattie asked.

"I don't have any money."

"You broke bitches ain't never got no money." She spat. I sighed restlessly. I was tired. I wasn't making much money at work, but I planned on saving all that I did make. I had to find a way out. After the incident with Dontay, I was determined to protect myself more. I vowed that I was never going to go through that again. I was tired of people hurting me, so I bought a gun.

CHAPTER ELEVEN

It had been a year, but not much was different at Grandma Hattie's. She was still cussing us out daily and the roach issue didn't resolve either. I tried my best not to complain. There was no need in complaining anyway. I didn't have a list of other options. So instead of focusing on what my circumstances were, I focused on things that I wanted to do and what I wanted my circumstances to become. At this point, I practically lived on my own. Grandma Hattie didn't care if I came or went, as long as I didn't bother her and as long as Toto was in the bed by 6pm.

"Hey girllll!" Shatia called out to me as I walked out of the school building at the end of the day. Shatia was a friend I had made over the summer after she saw me beat up a girl on Church and Frank Streets. She was cool and we got along well. She also knew my situation at Grandma Hattie's so much like Danisha's home, I spent a lot of time at Shatia's as well. "Stay the night at my house tonight so that we can go to the mall together tomorrow."

"That's cool. Just go with me to grab some clothes from my house." She called and asked her mother, Ms.

Vickie, if I could stay the night and if she could go with me to get my clothes. She said yes but we had to come straight to their house afterwards. She also instructed that I have a parent call her to assure that it was okay for me to stay the night. Once we reached my house to get my stuff, I hurried so that we wouldn't take long to get to Shatia's house. Once we made it to Shatia's house, I took a shower and changed into some relaxing clothes. Per usual, I enjoyed myself at her house. We listened to music and talked about everything under the sun until it was time for dinner.

"Come on girls. Let's eat before it gets late so I can take Sharda home." Vickie said.

"Ma. . ." Shatia started. "I asked if Sharda could stay the night here so we can go to the mall in the morning."

"Well, I also told you both to make sure an adult called me and that never happened so I'm taking her home. Just as I would have liked someone to do with you."

"But Ma. . ." Shatia whined.

"No buts. Call your parent right now Sharda or I'm going to take you home when you finish eating." Vickie said and handed me her cellphone.

"I can go home when I finish eating." I responded.

"Is there a reason why you can't call your parents?" Vickie asked. I had stopped eating and was silent for a minute before talking.

"I don't have anyone over me at home. There is no parent for you to call. My mother is not able to take care of me right now. I haven't seen my father. I was staying with my grandmother, but she has moved into a retirement home and the grandmother whose house I be at on North Street is always drunk and pays no attention to when I come or go. So, I'm on my own. I work as much as I can and take care of myself. Every now and then, my grandfather sends me money from Texas."

"Wow! I'm so sorry to hear that." Vickie said as tears welled in her eyes.

"But I understand your rules so I can go home." She didn't make me go home though. Ms. Vickie took me Grandma Hattie's house to get more clothes and stuff as she agreed that I could stay there for the rest of the week. It was fun to say the least. I felt that I had a normal life. Even if only for a week, I was fine with that. It was relieving. One day, Vickie came home from work and told me that she wanted to introduce me to someone.

"Denise, this is Sharda. Sharda, this is Denise. Denise is a young lady from my job." Ms. Vickie started.

"Hello, Denise" I spoke politely.

"Denise and her husband, Ray, doesn't have any children and would like to know how you would feel about them taking care of you. This is in no way, shape, or form some kind of charity or pity arrangement. Whole-heartedly, I believe that you all would fit well in each other's lives."

Vickie couldn't have been more right. I packed all of my stuff from Grandma Hattie's house and started staying with Denise and Ray soon after. They were so kind and treated me just like I was their daughter. I had my own room and my own bathroom. Ray would walk me to the bus stop every morning and Denise would cook dinner every day. We also ate dinner every night like a family. We would laugh and really have great conversations at the dinner tables;

discussing our days, sports, and anything I had upcoming in school. Denise packed me lunch daily, so Ray would take me to the store if needed to get things I needed for lunch or myself. He would always tell me, '*Keep going to school and doing the right thing and you're going to go far.*' I listened too, and I didn't give them any problems. I finally felt at peace. There was a lot of chaos in my life, but God always showed me a glimpse of hope and gave me a reason to keep a smile on my face.

CHAPTER TWELVE

Things were going great for a long while until they weren't. Denise began to get jealous of Ray's relationship with me. I had no idea why though because it was like a father and daughter and that was the purpose of them taking me in. I enjoyed having them both as parental figures but there was something about my connection to Ray that was not okay with Denise, and she let it be known. First, she grew more silent towards me. Then she became rude. One night before dinner, I was preparing to go downstairs, and I could hear her on the phone talking about me in her room.

"Yeah girl. . .His sorry ass wouldn't go to the store for me, but I bet you he would have went if Sharda asked him . . . Mmmhmmm. . .Yeah, I'm getting ready to because I'll be damned if I'm going to be uncomfortable in my own home. It's not going to happen." She continued until she heard my footsteps going down the steps. I made my way to the kitchen and took a seat at the table. I could hear Denise coming downstairs directly after.

"Hey baby girl." Ray greeted me cheerfully as he began to make my plate. He sat my plate in front of me and proceeded back to the stove.

"I'm your woman. Why didn't you make my plate?" Denise spat and Ray made her plate and sat it in front of her. We all ate dinner in silence. I went to bed early and even walked to the bus stop early so that Ray didn't walk me. I didn't know how much I could avoid Denise's resentment, but I didn't want to lose my happy place either.

The following day I was at work at McDonalds, and my godfather, Ramone came to get some food and saw me. We small talked for a little while about my circumstances and he told me to come over to the house so I could see my godmother and god sister. I decided it was a good idea as it would give Denise and Ray some time alone. It was refreshing to be in the presence of good company. We spent hours laughing and talking. I missed that in my own household. They also took me to the mall to buy me some clothes and stuff. Time had gotten away from us, so my god parents hurried to get me home. My godmother, Serena, had even sent Denise a text message. When I got there, I unlocked the door and pushed it open a little before waving goodbye to them. When they pulled off, I pushed the door and noticed that the chain lock was on the door. The chain lock never went on the door until I made it in the house. I knocked on the door and a few minutes later, Denise came to the door. She opened the door with the chain lock still attached.

"Hey! It's just me."

"I knew exactly who it was. Do you know what time it is?" She slurred, obviously drunk.

"Yes ma'am. Time got away from us. Serena sent you a text message when we were in route here." I explained.

"I didn't get any messages but let me give you one. No child under my roof in coming in at this hour. I'll see you tomorrow." She said to me sternly. I looked around her hoping that Ray would come to my aide, but I guess he was ducking her raft as well because I didn't hear any movement in the house at all.

"Come on Denise. Don't do this to me. Where am I supposed to go?" I pleaded.

"I don't know, and I don't care. Good night. See you tomorrow. Maybe then you will have some sense and come in at a decent hour." She said and slammed the door in my face. I looked around. I had no idea where I would go but I wasn't staying where I wasn't wanted either.

I didn't have a phone to call anyone, so I decided to walk across the street to the projects that sat on the opposite side of Denise's house. I knew a few people that lived over there but it seemed as if nobody was home. So, I roamed aimlessly through the projects for a while as it was cold sitting in one spot. It was getting later, and I was getting extremely tired. Just as I was about to walk out of the projects, I saw Aaron, a local d-boy I was cool with, and asked if I could use his phone. He obliged and at first, I had no idea who to call. Ultimately, I called Uncle Dirt and explained to him what happened, and he came to pick me up. By the time he got there, it was extremely late.

It was too late for me to go to Grandma Hattie's so he told me I could stay with him and go to Grandma Hattie's house in the morning. I didn't trust many people, so I only to Uncle Dirt a little bit about what was going on with me and what my plan was to fix it. Truth was that I didn't really have a plan, but I know Uncle Dirt had high expectations of me, so I came up with something. I just knew I wasn't at Denise and Ray's house anymore. We talked and ate and ended up falling asleep in the car. The next morning, he took me to get my stuff. It was crazy because Denise seemed sad that I was leaving even though she didn't mention it.

My stay with Grandma Hattie was short lived because I ended up moving in with my god parents, Serena and Ramone. They were really good to me the entire time I stayed with them. They had one daughter and she was like a little sister me. They treated us equal which I didn't even expect but when they bought one something, they bought something for the other one. They were very protective of us, but they weren't strict. So, I was able to go to sport games, activities, and events with my friends at school.

One night, I went to a championship basketball game with my Danisha, and everyone said we looked alike because we both long hair and wore glasses. The game was really hyped, and I ran into Kay, a lady I knew I from the neighborhood that always bought me stuff. I asked her for a ride home and she told me that she would have her son take me because she had something to do immediately after the game. Unbeknownst to me, her son was Scott, a star player of the basketball team.

He was so easy to talk to and we hit it off immediately. We talked about basketball and what he planned to do with his career as a player since he was a senior and one of the best basketball players in Michigan. I didn't think that Scott knew me, so it surprised me when he knew that me and my homegirl, Tasha, were the only freshman to make the varsity team. Scott had been on the news and in newspapers because his team was the best high school basketball team in the state. They were undefeated and made it to the regional games. When Scott dropped me off, he walked me to my door, and we found out that night that Ramone and Scott were cousins. Needless to say, we really started kicking it after that because he was always welcome to come over.

CHAPTER THIRTEEN

Though I loved staying with my god parents, I was ecstatic when Grandma decided to move back into The Rowhouses on Florence. I was even happier to move back in with her and it was just me, her, and Donnie. I had been sick for a few days, so I was in bed for the entire weekend. I was about a month pregnant and already having morning sickness. One morning I got up for school, before I could place my feet on the ground, I felt like I had to throw up. I ran in the bathroom and turned the water on while I threw up in the toilet. When I was done throwing up, I put my back against the door and slid down it. I put my face down in my hands because I knew if Grandma found out, she would kill me. Grandma called me on it, but I lied and told her that it was something I ate.

"I ain't no damn fool!" she said.

"Grandma, you tripping!" I don't think she bought that, but she didn't mention it again. I didn't know what I wanted to do yet. My reservations included the fact that I was not finished school and barely stable, Scott was almost finished with high school and headed to college, and I didn't want to raise my baby in Kalamazoo.

Outside of Scott, Tiffany and Mary were the first people to know. Tiffany was excited but I felt Mary was disappointed. Mary was pregnant as well and bout the same number of weeks as me. They kept it as secret for me and didn't tell anyone. It felt good to have my girls to talk to about it in addition to Scott. One day while we were eating dinner, I decided to let Grandma know in my own way.

"Grandma, I have a question."

"What is it?"

"Do you believe in abortions?"

"That's a tough question. I wouldn't say I don't believe in them. I would say it honestly didn't matter what I was believed. It's about what the pregnant woman believes and what she decides for herself, her body, and her future."

"I'm pregnant and I want to get an abortion." I blurted out to get it over with.

"Have you thought about it? You know that's a big decision and not just a small thing that can be reversed."

"Yeah, I thought about it." How could I bring a child into this cruel world, and I had nothing to offer it? I also didn't ruin Scott's future.

"Well, make the appointment. I'll take you." She sighed. If I wasn't mistaken, it would appear that she was disappointed. On the morning of my appointment, I wasn't able to get the abortion because Grandma had misplaced the paperwork. So, I took that as a sign to keep my baby. Unbeknownst to me, that would be the best thing that happened to me. It was scary because I felt like I wasn't going to be able to take care of my baby like I wanted to, but I had decided to stop thinking negatively. I may not have been in the best of conditions, but I certainly wasn't in the worst either.

One day, I was using the bathroom and heard a bunch of commotion and screaming outside of the bathroom window, so I looked out. Our bathroom's window faced Florence Street, and as I look out of it toward Burrell Street, there was a lady getting beat on by her pimp. As he beat on her like he was fighting a grown man, he repeatedly yelled, "Where is my fucking money?" My heart ached for her, and I wanted to help her so bad but where I'm from, you have to mind your business. It was an unspoken law. The next day, the police were canvassing the neighborhood inquiring about the whereabouts of the lady that was getting beat in the alley the day before. Her family had reported her missing. Once they reached our door, they weren't even able to complete the sentence. Grandma didn't play talking to no police under any circumstances.

"We don't know shit. Get the hell away from my damn door!" She yelled as she instructed me to close the door. While there weren't many things, I had figured out about being a mom, I knew I didn't want to raise my baby in Kalamazoo for sure.

CHAPTER FOURTEEN

My belly was growing, and it was no secret that I was pregnant at this point. I had even found out that I was having a son. One night, my sister, her friend, and I were sitting in my sister's car out back of Grandma's house. It had been a while since I was outside, so I was enjoying myself. J-Rock, a long-time friend from the neighborhood that I had lost my virginity to when I was 14, was leaning in my window, talking to me.

"You know you're always going to be my baby, right?" He said looking in my eyes.

"Boy, shut up." I said as I hit him playfully.

"For real. Let me know if you need anything for the baby. I got you." He said and winked. "Sharda, can y'all go get me a #7 from McDonalds?"

"Yeah, I don't care." I responded and he handed me the money.

"What kind of soda?" I asked.

"Hi-C Orange." We went and got his food and returned about 20 minutes later.

By the time we came back, everyone was outside and all of the drive ways were filled with cars and people. Everyone was talking, laughing, playing around, listening to music, and just chilling. We sat on the hood of the car and listened to our music that we were playing. J-Rock, Pumpkin, Lor Roy, Lor Corey, and Meter were all talking amongst themselves when a car pulled up on them and the occupants started talking shit. Lil Roy started talking shit back to them and going towards the car, but J-Rock held his hand up in front of Lil Roy stopping him. "Chill. We not on that shit tonight." J-Rock said to Lil Roy. The car pulled off and when it got to the corner, an occupant of the car let off one shot in the air and all hell broke loose. Gunfire erupted from everywhere. Pumpkin grabbed me and pulled me down to the ground and laid over top of me. I kept my eyes closed as the gunfire continued to sound off. You could hear the wheels of a car pulling off fast as it ceased. Breathing a sigh of relief, I opened my eyes and couldn't believe them. J-Rock was staring me right in my eyes.

"You okay Sharda?" Pumpkin asked but I couldn't respond. I was speechless. He followed my eyes and realized that J-rock had been shot. Pumpkin and many others ran to his aid, but I was in so much shock, I ran towards the house. Everyone was taking off their white t-shirts and applying pressure to his gunshot wounds. Even with all of their shirts stacked together, the blood seeped through profusely. Someone called the ambulance, but it was too late when they arrived. I couldn't believe that my childhood friend was laying on the ground dead. It felt like the whole world stopped but of course it didn't because so many people were showing up. Chaos erupted, so the paramedics told us that they would do their best to work on him. Sadly, we knew that he was gone because they didn't even turn on the sirens as they left. The whole hood was sad, and the pain hurt even more when it was officially announced that he was deceased. Mary came over and told me the news, but I already knew and still couldn't believe it. What a beautiful soul to take so young? In need of fresh air, I went to leave out with Mary but when I opened the back door, I was stuck. Standing there for a minute, I let a single tear fall down my face. His blood was still splattered on the pavement and the yellow tape was still hanging. Seeing the scene broke my heart all over again. That moment changed my life forever. Closing the back door, I decided to leave out through the front. It was then that I vowed to myself that I wasn't raising my son in Kalamazoo. I had to make a plan and work the plan because staying wasn't an option for us.

con•vic•ted
/kən'viktəd/

Adjective
1. having been declared guilty of an offense

Beauty, class, rarity, and style are the epitome of conversations around diamonds. What does it go thought to be beautiful? A diamond is convicted to 2500 degrees Fahrenheit and 825,000 pounds per square inch in pressure, a little bit of carbon, and the diamond seed to provide the foundation in order to form a raw diamond. With that information, can you see why diamonds are considered a "girl's best friend?" There is the chance for similar stories,

maybe even shared circumstances, but in no way are

two diamonds ever alike; neither are the

incarceration experiences of two women. Well, here

is mine. . .

CHAPTER FIFTEEN

As I sat in the interrogation room, it seemed to be getting colder and colder as time passed. Exhaustion and hunger pains were setting in, but I was aware that the detectives who have been interrogating me were doing these things in an attempt to break my silence. It wouldn't work though. So, I sat there alone for hours at a time between detectives coming in and out. Like clockwork, after about 3 hours, a new detective walked in. Each of the ones before him was loud, disrespectful, got in my face, threw books of paper and pens, and told me to write a statement. One even grabbed me by my arm, twisted it, and even put the handcuffs on me very tight. I sat in pain for three hours until the next detective came in.

"Dominica Sharda Sims, correct?" He asked as he sat down. I gave him my attention but maintained my silence. "Look, I'm not here to play games with you. Where were you on the night in question?" Silence. "Okay." The detective smirked before continuing. "See, I was trying to give you a chance to tell me your side of the story but your friend – or should I say co-defendant – she's in the next room spilling her guts so I really don't *need* you to talk at all. You'll only making it worse for yourself. But before I leave, just listen." He pressed play on the recorded.

"She made us do it! I'm telling you we had no choice! She came up with the entire plan and forced us to help her! We tried to back out several time, but she said she'd handle us if we did, and we didn't want to go there with her! I'm telling you! No one does. She is a different person when she's mad." A familiar voice lied blatantly as if she was in distress.

"And by she, you're referring to Dominica Sims?" A male's voice asked.

The detective stopped the tape and I put my head down.

"It's fine. You don't have to talk" The detective picked up the recorder and stood up. "You won't see your son again outside of prison!"

"I need to make a call." I spoke for the first time. "I know I get a phone call. I need to make it." There was a phone in the interrogation room and the detective allowed me to use it. Without a second thought, I called Grandma and told her my charges.

"Oh, my Lord. What in the world? I told you stay away from them no good ass girls. You just wouldn't listen to me. You need a good lawyer for those charges. We cannot afford no lawyer. What are we going to do? Lordddd!" I listened in silence as I fought the tears that dared to drop from my eyes. "I tell you one thing. Pick your head up right now!" She demanded as if she could see me through the phone. I don't know what happened because I wasn't there, but I know you and who you are and who I raised you to be." When we little, Grandma always took us to church, and we had really strong faith in God. In this moment, I knew that

God was the only one that could help me. "Pray every single day. Do you hear me? Every single day!" I hung up the phone. I knew they were watching me behind the plexiglass in hopes of me incriminating myself.

"I want a lawyer!" I shouted. Without delay, a female detective handcuffed me and prepared me to be transported to jail. During the ride, there was no noise outside of a woman's voice reporting crime scenes over the dispatching system. I didn't talk to either of the deputies who transported me, nor did they say anything to me. That was perfectly fine with me as we didn't have anything to discuss. We were stopped by county sheriffs as we approached the county jail.

"Good afternoon officers. You will have to park and wait in the secure parking lot, and we'll let you know when you can bring the inmate in."

"Damn! Do you know how long it's going to be?" The deputy who was driving asked the sheriff.

"There's no approximate time frame but it may take a few hours." They complained but we sat in the parking lot for an hour before I was allowed to come in and be processed. The jail was dirty, and the intake process was one of the most degrading experiences a human can encounter. Before a judge or jury can decide your innocence or guilt, you are immediately viewed and treated like a criminal. Initially, I was placed in the holding tank. There were women there from many different walks of life. There was a single bench in the room, but there was only space for four people on it. There was about 25 of us in there at the time. There was one toilet that sat in the corner of the room, but it was stopped up and smelled so horrible. I felt completely out of place. Cringing, I stood as still as possible because I didn't want anyone to touch me.

"KK, get off that bench and let that baby sit down!" A lady, arrested for prostitution, said to a lady sitting on the bench. KK mumbled something but she got up and took a seat on the floor. "Go on and sit down, baby." She said looking at me. I took a seat and nodded my head in thanks to her. "You don't look like you belong here." She said as she walked up to me. "Don't tell anyone what you're arrested for or any information about your case because they'll use it against you."

The first night was the worse. I was starving and dehydrated as I literally hadn't eaten or drank anything in 24 hours. After I was taken to my cell, a tray was brought to my cell. I couldn't even begin to tell you what it was supposed to be because I had no idea what it was myself. I did get a water and that's what I decided to consume before I dozed off. Unable to sleep, I sat up on my bunk and leaned my head back on the wall.

"Sims." A male officer said.

"Yeah. That's me." I responded.

"Seventeen? Murder? You have your whole life ahead of you." He said softly. I didn't respond. I just put my head down. "I'm not judging. Come on. Your lawyer is here to see you." Confused, I allowed him to lead me to a small room where a white, middle-aged man sat at a table filled with papers.

"Hello. How are you Ms. Sims? My name is Daniel Lee and am an attorney from the Public Defender's Office." The lawyer introduced himself as I was led to sit across from him. I nodded my head to greet him. "So, I take it you don't talk much and that's okay. Uuhhh. . . Let's see. You have officially been charged as an adult on both felony charges. So, there's two options. Obviously, you can take it to trial but there is also a plea agreement on the table." I didn't fully understand the specifics of the legal stuff he was saying because he was speaking too fast. Also, I had no idea what a plea was.

"I'm going to trial." I stated matter-of-factly.

"I thought that you would say that. Ms. Sims. . ."

"Dominica is fine."

"Dominica, I have reviewed the evidence. It would take a miracle for you to win this case."

"And it will take guilt for me to lose it. I'm going to trial. The evidence they have won't stand because they are lying, adding stuff, and exaggerating things. They have all the information wrong." I raised my voice.

"There's no need to yell. You have every right to go to trial. The decision is yours. I'm here to help you make the best decision for your life. Understand this you have a newborn son. If you go to trial and lose, you risk doing life in prison with the possibility of no parole. Take the plea and serve 30 years. . ."

"THIRTY YEARS?!"

"Yes, thirty years or less with good behavior but you will live to see your son on the outside again."

"I'm not taking no damn thirty years." My voice cracked. "I'm going home to my son."

"Alright! I will let the D.A. know that you will not take the plea and I will prepare for trial.

"You still didn't ask me."

"Excuse me." Daniel stopped packing his bag and gave me his attention.

"You haven't asked me if I'm guilty of what they're charging me with."

"Because it's not about if you're innocent or guilty. It's about what can be proven beyond a reasonable doubt in a court of law. This isn't the juvenile justice system. This is the big league." His words echoed in my head as I laid on my bunk.

"Sims. . ." The officer who walked me to meet my lawyer said to me as he stood at my gate, but I didn't respond. "Listen, I don't know if you are sleep but if you aren't, I want you to stay strong. Don't clique up with these women and make sure you get your education. When you are incarcerated, they strip you of everything, but they cannot strip you of the knowledge you gain. Every program they have that interests you, take it. Contrary to popular belief, to survive prison, you must keep your mind sharp, make decisions with your head and not your heart. I won't lie and say this won't be hard but you're going to be okay."

"Thank you." I said softly as I heard his footsteps walking away from my cell.

"You're more than welcome." He called back. I closed my eyes and then my bunk buddy, Ms. Anne started talking to me.

"He's a good officer. Kind. Respectful. Knowledgeable. It's a shame that the other officers aren't like that." She paused before continuing. "Tonya's your mother, isn't she?"

"How do you know my mom?" I sat up and asked. Ms. Anne went on to explain how my mom and herself were good friends and said my mom talked about us all the time. She informed me that my mom never went without saying she loved us so much. We talked about my mom for a long while before she concluded our conversation for her to go to bed.

"I have been to prison before and that is something you have to prepare yourself for. If by chance you have to go to prison, no matter how much time you have to do, make sure you stay focused on getting home. The day you go to prison is the day you need to start preparing for when you go home. Act like your first day in prison is your last day in prison. People that go to prison, comes out three ways; worse person, better person, or the same person. It's rare that you find a genuine person in there. It's not impossible but don't be gullible. You're young and seem to have a good head on your shoulders. Utilize every resource they have for you to maximize your success when leave. Now, goodnight. My meds have kicked in and I have to get some rest."

"Good night Ms. Anne." I laughed because I noticed that many people used the sleeping meds, they had at med lines to help them sleep at night. That was the first of many life-changing conversations that I would have with Ms. Anne. She helped me get through so many lonely and depressive days while I was in county.

CHAPTER SIXTEEN

After I was sentenced, I was transported from the city jail to Robert Scott Correctional Facility. The intake officer was mean, rough, and very aggressive and did a lot of yelling. I was relieved to finally make it to a cell, but my guard was up. My bunky was not in the room when I first got to my cell. After a few days, I got acclimated to my surroundings. Robert Scott's was completely different than the county jail. After leaving intake, I went to healthcare. That's where I met Tonya. Tonya gave me a big package that contained t-shirts, socks, food, and snacks. She was a lifer who knew my mom from them doing time together. She took me under her wing and became my "Prison Mom." Her sharing the same name as my mom and showing major respect to my mom made it easier for me to let my guard down a bit. Tonya wasn't the one to play with, but she was very compassionate towards me, and I believe it was because I was so young. Quickly, I adapted the name Lil Baby because of my age. Every day, Tonya would come to my window and talk to me. *'If you need anything at all, just let me know. I will get it for you.'* She would say this to me daily. I knew that she was sincere because she had major prison clout. I was on quarantine for my first week, so the only way I was able to leave my cell was to go to healthcare. Tonya had it arranged with Mr. W, a prison officer, that I would get called to healthcare a few times a week just so I can get some time outside of my cell.

Mr. W became like a brother to me. He always offered me advice when I went to healthcare. *'Make education a priority while you're in here. Never stop learning. Take as many classes as you can and, also get in that law library. Study the law and your case. Stay out the way and get out of here early. Don't get in here messing with women and calling yourself in no relationship because these women will chew you up and spit you out and go on to a new victim. I've seen it too many times before.'* He easily became one of my favorite prison officers. While they have a job to do and some can be mean and aggressive for no reason, there were officers like Mr. W who still treated us as women and not animals.

After three months, I had to go to close custody. Close custody was a mixture of inmates doing nine months & a day and inmates with behavioral issues. The struggle was real. I saw so many unimaginable things happen while I was in close custody. There were so many fights, people getting set up, people getting beat up and cut up, and people being taken advantage of. We were locked down the majority of the day. There was this one girl named Teal Dean whom I met and became cool with. In conversation, we found out that she knew my mom so she would talk to me about her. Teal owned a lot of jewelry and gave me a gold ring because she loved my mom. One day, she got into it with some girls over some money from a pinochle game. Their plan was to jump her, but they had a rude awakening because she could fight really good. Me and Teal was sitting on base, on the exercise machines when we saw them coming. Teal was already on point, as she had just told me that she was expecting them to come and fight her. She beat them both up at the same time. While she was beating up the one of the girls, the other girl hit Tia in the eye with a lock. Her eye immediately busted open, and blood was squirting everywhere. I had never seen anything like that before, but Teal kept fighting.

Before I went to close custody, Tonya told me about Cyp, one of her other prison kids. Cyp was on segregation, but was released to Auburn B, which is where I was also housed. Tonya arranged for us to meet and Cyp and I clicked from the first day we met. Cyp was a lifer as well, but she was a sweetheart and all the ladies in the prison loved her. From day one, she treated me just like I was her little sister. She nicknamed me the Princess of the family. Every day, Cyp and I would walk the track and talk about everything. She often expressed how she felt that I didn't belong in prison with all those women and how that she couldn't wait for me to go home. The burden on my heart from missing Lil Scott was something I would talk with Cyp about, and she would always comfort me. She would reassure me that I would be home with him one day.

"Give me a contact so that I can send Lil Scott some money." She said one day while we were walking the track.

"Nahh. You don't have to do that. I appreciate it though."

"I'm not asking. We're family and we all we got. So, I need that contact information as soon as possible." She demanded. I gave her the contact information for Big Scott's I, and just as she said, she began sending her money for Lil Scott. While I appreciated what Cyp was doing, I wanted to put myself in position to take care of my own son. So, another day when we were walking the track, I told Cyp that I wanted to make some money for myself. She looked at me and like a true big sister she explained to me that she wasn't having it. *'For as long as you are inside these walls, do as I say and not as I do. I got you. You just go to school and finish your diploma and go to college. Don't worry about no money. I'mma get the money.'* She was true to her word.

Once my visitation was approved, I called Grandma and asked her and Aunt Meka to come see me. On the day of their visit, I was excited because they were bringing Lil. Scott with them. We talked often, but he hadn't seen me since the day that I was initially arrested so I was experiencing all types of thoughts and emotions. I busied myself preparing. I wanted my clothes and hair to be neat and freshly pressed. When they first arrived, I hugged Lil Scott so tight. Then I hugged Grandma and Aunt Meka. During visits, your relatives are allowed to buy you snacks and Pop that can be consumed during the visit, so they loaded me down. We sat at the table talking and catching up, Lil Scott sat on my lap, rubbing his little fingers across my face and my hair. He was two years of age now, so he was walking and talking up a storm in his own little language. I remember Kim, Ayanna and Eisha's mom, telling me that when I had my visit with Lil Scott to lay his head on my chest so he could hear my heart beat.

"Ewww!" I said as he backwashed in my Pop.

"That's your son, girl!" Aunt Meka exclaimed, and we all laughed, even Lil Scott. Shortly after the laughter, I felt sad. Aunt Meka's words echoed in my head. *'That's your son, girl! That's your son, girl!'*

"What you thinking, Sharda?" Grandma asked, noticing my mood shift.

"Disappointed in myself, honestly." I admitted. I know I broke my grandmother's heart with making a bad decision and ending up in prison. She did a great job raising us.

"*ALL* have sinned and fallen short of the glory of God. You pick yourself up and do not let this defeat you. You gonna be alright. I got you and your baby loves you. Most importantly, God got you. He is in charge and in control!" Grandma encouraged me.

"You are currently a diamond in the rough. You're going to come out of this shining. Watch what I tell you." Aunt Meka said reassuringly. It was getting close to the end of the visit, so we prayed. Afterwards, I felt a little better, but I still yearned to get back home to my son. Once the visits had concluded, all inmates had to remain seated while the visitors left. Aunt Meka and Grandma got their coats on while I snuck in a few more kisses and hugs with Lil Scott. I didn't want to let him go but I knew I had to as I didn't want to take any chances of getting my visits taken. Watching them leave was a hurting feeling. As they neared the exit, Lil Scott stopped and turned around.

"Come on Mommy. Let's go." He called out to me while motioning his hand for me to come with him. My heart broke and in that moment, I felt a pain that I could not describe.

"Come on baby. Mommy can't go right now. Okay?" Aunt Meka said while picking Lil Scott up and looking at me with tears in her eyes. In fact, there wasn't a dry eye in the room. Other inmates and the visitors who were leaving were all in tears. Even the prison officer had tears in her eyes. Once all the visitors were gone, the prison officer allowed me to get strip searched first. I hated the strip search process, but seeing my son made it all worth it. While getting strip searched, I couldn't help but to cry. The prison officer, Ms.

Mason wiped, her eyes and told me that she had a three-year-old son and couldn't imagine being in my position.

"Sims, I want you to know I will be praying for you as long as you are in this place." Ms. Mason said to me upon completion of the strip search. That was one of the worst days of my entire sentence. I laid in my bed and couldn't sleep that night. I felt terrible. How could I do this? How could I leave my son out in the world all alone? By the end of the night, I felt really motivated to get focused. More determined than ever, I was certain that I was going to go home a better person and a better mom. Within the first six months of being in prison, I earned my GED, and realized I actually enjoyed educating myself. My family visits kept me motivated and reassured me that I had people counting to come home. It still was hard to see them leave but as time passed, I handled it better.

Cyp remained supportive. Daily, she would pick me up from school, before we would walk the track. She had a girlfriend, T.M. and we would stop by her window to see her on our walks. One day while we were talking to T.M., I told Cyp that I wanted to go in because my feet were cold. T.M. started yelling at me so I thought she was mean and didn't like her anymore. Soon after the siren went off, the prison was under mobilization, and we were put on lock down.

CHAPTER SEVENTEEN

After a year in close custody, they were forcing me to go on grounds, so I moved in a room with Tonya. In medium custody, they days were a lot longer because we had a lot more time to ourselves. I started signing to go on more call outs and getting actively involved in more groups. Often times, I would go over to the gym for rec to play basketball and skate. Every Friday, I met T.M., Auntie Lawanda, and Geneva Archie over there to skate. They taught me how to skate backwards.

One day, right before the unit locked up, Yulonda, an inmate I socialized with asked if she could speak with me. Yulanda worked in the intake center where Tonya, my prison mom, used to work. She was cool so I stepped off to talk to her.

"Your mom was in intake today." She informed me.

"Damn. For real?" I asked disappointedly.

"Yes. So, come to chow so I can take you to the control center to see her."

"Okay. I will. Thank you." I waited anxiously on my bed for the count to clear which seemed to be taken particularly long on this specific day. When I got to the control center, Officer Carvell that was walking with my mom and turned his back so that I could hug her. That hug seemed to be a need for both of us at the time because we both felt so much refuge in it. I was also able to give my mom the personals I smuggled over there for her while reminding her to stay low and out of trouble and promising to see her again soon.

A short time later, I was moved to Women's Huron Valley Correctional Facility, because the Warden ordered a Keep Separate Spon between me and my mom. Not only was I sad that I had to leave Scotts, but Huron Valley was the prison my maternal grandmother died in. When I first got there, I would stare out of my window for hours just thinking about her, hoping she would give me a sign that she was there watching over me. I wondered how she felt spending the last days of her life incarcerated and eventually dying there. Though I could vaguely remember details about her, I remembered her funeral vividly.

I remember everyone getting dressed to go to the funeral except me as I wasn't allowed to attend. As the black cars lined up out front, my grandmother's funeral started to look like a car show. There were so many people, and everyone was dressed to impress. Women and men both came out in their flyest furs and finest jewelry. That came as no surprise because I would always hear stories about my grandmother, and how fly and infamous she was. I'm sure that's where my mother got it from. What was even more memorable about her funeral was that people were grieving authentically. The city of Kalamazoo had suffered a significant loss and the real came out to pay their respect.

"Hey girl! What you thinking about?" Pam asked as her and Chanika came to my cell to get me before we went to the day room. Pam was my prison mom, Tonya's prison sister and Chanika was Pam's bunky. Chanika and I became really good friends. She would always come by and talk to me.

"Just thinking about my grandmother again." I responded softly.

"Your grandmother is your angel now. She passed away in this same building so her spirit is surely with you, and I know she is so proud. Look at what all you have accomplished. She's bragging to God about you Domo. Come on out of this cell and go to the day room with us." Pam said to me encouragingly. I obliged. As we walked to the day room, there were transactions happening left and right without regard. People were passing drugs and commissary as currency. Inmates came and went in their units as they pleased. The structure was more chaotic than Scotts. This is where I learned how to really jail. There was so much freedom at Huron Valley, so I learned a lot about the prison drug trade. The most valuable items in prison were food, cigarettes, stamps, and extra phone time.

On my way to lunch, I saw Starr, another inmate I had grown close to. I met Starr on her ride in. When she arrived at the prison, she put the word out that she was looking for me. A friend of ours who was still at Scotts, told her to look for me and stick close to me. We clicked the first day we met and spent a lot of time together. Once we were in the chow hall, we waited on our queue to go and pick up our kitchen goods which was considered contraband from the kitchen worker. The kitchen worker made sure the goods were covered in layers of saran wrap because we had to stuff the wrapped goods in our clothes; in our pants, under our breasts, or wherever we could to get them pass the officers.

Quickly, I had gotten a job as a tutor and was assigned a non-smoking room. However, after four months, I was moved back to Robert Scott's. When I returned there was a big mobilization because a prison officer lost his gun clip. The warden brought in the Michigan Correctional SWAT Team, and they search out rooms for the lost clip. They were throwing our things around and tearing our stuff up looking for the lost gun clip and confiscating any contraband they found. I was getting my hair pressed in the grooming room when the search started. So, when the mobilization siren sounded signaling for us to leave the grooming room, I was irritated because you only had a certain amount of time to get your hair done. As the prison officers began to put up the hair tools and cosmetic stuff, I grabbed a roll of tissue and went into the bathroom, but it was crowded. There were only 4 stalls which were all occupied and 8 women waiting to use one. Though some of us had to use the bathroom, it would have to wait because there were others flushing and stuffing their drugs. It was complete chaos. Inmates were running everywhere. They tore the cells up completely and one by one we were strip searched in the laundry room on a cardboard box. Afterwards, we were on lockdown for a week. The day of the search, they locked Cyp up.

CHAPTER EIGHTEEN

The prison could move you whenever they felt like it, so it was no surprise that I ended up getting moved back to Huron Valley again. While I was sad to leave Cyp, I was happy to have Starr, Pam, and Chanika. Plus, my mom was incarcerated again and housed there. She was in the infirmary having my baby brother when I arrived, so I was unable to see her immediately.

One particular night, I was in my room watching The First 48 and they were investigating the murder of a young man in Memphis named Jeremy "J-Rock" Young. I couldn't believe my ears – the young man had the same name as my friend J-Rock, down to the nickname. Chills went through my body. *Rest in peace J-Rock.* I thought to myself.

For the most part, I was either in the day room or on a call out. I was signed up for college and I was involved in a lot of groups. There were people that I associated with, but I spent most of time doing something productive. That didn't stop drama from coming my way. These girls got into it with some girls I was cool and because I was the smallest, I felt like they called themselves bullying me. At first, I ignored them because they were really all bark. However, they caught me on a bad day. I choked one of them really bad, and the others didn't budge. I never had a problem with them again. Thankfully, I wasn't caught because I would have been sent straight to segregation. To blow off some steam, Angel P. and I snuck to get a tattoo in the bathroom. I got Lil Scott's name.

"Sims!" Ms. B, a prison officer, called out to me on my way to the day room, motioning for me to come to the officer's booth. Ms. B was real cool like a sister.

"What's up B?"

"You know these walks talk. What are you doing fighting?'' I didn't respond so she continued. "Stay out of trouble and stay true to yourself. Don't let your incarceration change you. They couldn't wait to drop a kite on you for real. You got to stay out of the way. They thought I was going to lock you up but I'm not locking nobody up off no snitch kite."

"Sure thing." I said as I walked away. I was starting to hate these women. They were so jealous, evil, and conniving.

A few days later I was sitting in the day room, I got word that Cyp was at Huron Valley. I sat in the day room window and waited for her to pull her property down the walkway. When we reunited, it instantly made me happier. She had so many grandfather items for us. She brought me so many clothes, underwear, and food items to last me for a long time. After a while, the presence of the prison officers grew so the money stopped coming in. We were down bad – like real bad – down to our last. At least I know I was. I was down to my last bar of soap, last deodorant, and last tube of toothpaste – which was very unusual for me. I didn't know where I was going to get stuff from because I didn't have store coming, didn't have a job, and no one had sent me any money. I knew I had to figure something out. Cyp and I sat in the day room talking before the unit closed. We were both sad, depressed, and felt like giving up.

"Man, fam, I'm so hungry." Cyp said.

"Me too. I'm starving."

"All I have is one noodle." Cyp said.

"You're doing better than me. I don't even have a noodle."

Before the unit closed, we ran to our rooms and got our bowls and cooked the noodle. Cyp took two forks full of the noodles and put it in her bowl and put the rest in mine. We knew it would at least take the edge off our stomachs until the next day. As we walked back to our rooms, I looked at Cyp.

"We're all we got fam." I said to her. One thing about being locked up, you have to keep your faith. *Something is going to happen.* Two days after we shared that last noodle, we were back getting money. Out of all the time we were up, it was the time that we were down bad that really bonded us. I fell asleep praying and thanking God that I had a genuine friend. Suddenly, I was awakened from my sleep, but it felt like someone was holding me down. I was conscious but I couldn't move. This scared me and it hard for me to sleep for days because I didn't know what that was.

New Years' was approaching and we wanted to have a party. Two of the warehouse workers lived in my unit and I asked them if I sent some stuff to the warehouse, could they smuggle it back into the prison. They said yes and I paid them for three trips. On the day that the third trip was supposed to come in, they pulled a mobilization and the warehouse officer found all of the contraband. This bust made the prison hot, but we were still able to have our New Years' party because we buried the contraband from the first two trips on the small yard.

CHAPTER NINETEEN

She thinks she's all that. Always with Cyp. They're probably fucking. I don't know who she thinks she is. All day every day these same group of girls threw their slurs or laughed when I walked pass. I always kept it moving like they didn't even exist. One day, I was on my way to see Chanika and Keisha. Keisha was cool and thought I was the cutest little thing in the world. While on my way, one of the nitpicking girls walked in front of me in the same direction. She went through the door that led to their side and closed the door in my face.

"Oh, I'm sorry. I didn't see you." She apologized sarcastically and smirked after I opened the door immediately after she closed it.

"You saw me!" I retorted. "I'm going to beat one of them bitches ass! Keep playing with me. Watch! Won't none of their asses be laughing then!" I shouted as I as soon as I entered their room.

"Who?" Chanika inquired. "Them bitches downstairs?"

"Yes! But I don't care who they are. They are going to stop fucking playing with me."

"Fuck them."

"Fuck who?" Cyp said as she appeared at the door to get me for our daily walk.

"Nobody. Come on." I said brushing it off. Cyp had already told me don't pay them any mind, so I didn't want to discuss it with her. I promised her I would stay focused. We did our daily walk, and I made my way back to my room. Lil Scott's 5th birthday was approaching, and it made me sad that I wasn't home to celebrate it with him.

"Good morning, my little princess. What do you want to do for Lil Scott's birthday?" Cyp asked as she entered my room on the morning of his birthday.

"Nothing, I just want to call him." I responded. Cyp had already put $100 on my phone account. Calls were ten cents per minute so I could talk to him as long as I wanted to, and this made me happy.

"Enjoy your call and send my love. Meet me at the walkway at 2:30pm." Cyp said before walking off. I took a deep breath as the phone rang.

"Hey Sharda. How are you?" Lil Scott's grandmother asked me.

"I'm okay. How are you"

"I'm blessed. Hold on." She responded. "Scotttt! Come get the phone baby. Mommy's on the phone."

"Hello Mommy. I miss you."

"Hey baby! I miss you more."

"It's my birthday Mommy."

"I know it's your birthday. You're growing up on me. What are you doing for your birthday?"

"I'm having a party. Can you come to my party Mommy?"

"I can't make it to the party baby." My voice threatened to crack. "But soon, one day I will celebrate with you and we're going to have so much fun. Okay?" I never promised to make up for anything as we all know time waits for no one and once that time is gone, you'll never get it back.

"Okay. I have a big cake."

"You do. That's amazing. Can you eat some cake for me too?"

"Yes, so I can have two slices of cake. Grandma!" He called out. "My Mommy said I can eat two pieces of cake. One for me and one for her. Okay, Grandma." I used the duration of my morning time out to talk to Lil Scott without any interruption. I was happy to talk to him and extremely sad when I had to end the call. I went to my room and cried myself to sleep. When it was time to go out again, I didn't want to get out of my bed, but I had already told Cyp that I would meet her at the 2:30 walkway. Cyp had surprised me with a cheesecake for Lil Scott's birthday. I was happy and really appreciated her.

"Since you couldn't make the party *this time*, we're going to have our own party for him." Cyp said and went out to the yard to celebrate. We enjoyed our dessert and conversation. "Princess, you have an out date so don't get comfortable in here. You are the hope for all of us when you get out of here. You are smart and you always got something going for yourself. You're going to get out of here and be so great. So, please stay out of trouble and don't worry about small stuff. You feel me?"

"Yeah. I do."

"Keep your head up always. Just stay out of trouble, do your time, and go home to your baby. Do not get put in segregation for any reason because nothing is worth it. You know that pain you felt when you had to end your call with Lil Scott? Keep that feeling up front. Every time you're about to make a bad decision, consider if it's worth not going home to him. Make sure you write your book like you said. I can't wait for it to come out. You have a story and it's going to be a blessing to many young girls and old ones too. Accomplish all of your goals. Lil Scott is your motivation. Make him proud."

"I am, for sure. I'm not going to involve myself in anything unnecessarily." I said and I meant that. As long as them bitches stayed out of my way, I would be good.

"Good because we have a lot of stuff coming and we have to keep our areas clean. Ms. W going to make sure she let us know when a mobilization will happen."

"Okay, cool. I can't believe you still messing with her." I said and we both laughed. Ms. W was a prison officer that was in love with Cyp. She did not play about Cyp. She was running up on inmates that she thought Cyp was dealing with telling them to stay away from Cyp.

As things started to get back to normal with Cyp and I, there seemed to be a bad omen over the prison. There was a lot of fights. Many of the women were depressed. There was also so much tension. I tried my best to stay out of the way, but unfortunately, I still found myself in some type of trouble.

"What y'all wanna do?" I asked as I walked up to the bitch that was always talking. I stood face to face with her. "What the fuck do you wanna do because I'm tired of talking?" I pointed in her face, asking again. The girls still wanted to go on and on fussing.

"Go to the unit." Cyp said grabbing me and pushing me towards the unit. "Ain't nobody else doing shit. You're the only one that want to fight. They don't want to fight. They ain't going to do shit! Go to the unit now!" I walked off going towards my unit and ran into T.M.

"Why you looking like that?" T.M. asked.

"I'm boutta fight."

"Noooo! Don't do it. It's not worth it. They're just jealous."

"I'm fighting regardless." I stopped in my tracks and looked T.M. in the face. "I'm tired of this shit." As we stood there in the hallway, the group of girls walked in towards us. As I was saying What's Up, I popped the first one that walked in the door. I beat her ass until the officers broke it up and took us back to the unit. Then, I reached around the officers and slapped her again.

It was no surprise that I was taken to segregation. For the first 24 hours, every time they opened the door, I was looking for my people because I knew that they were going to whip the rest of those bitches' asses. None of my people ever came through those doors. I made a vow to myself right then and there that I was never fighting for anyone and that I would just worry about myself moving forward. Though I beat her ass, I was still mad that I had been in a fight. This was my first time in segregation. Though I could still have visits in segregation, I didn't want my son to visit me through the glass. So, I wrote home to let my family know not to bring Lil Scott to see me. I was so disappointed in myself. I promised myself that I would try my best to never get in a fight again because even though I felt that bitch had it coming, I realized nothing was worth me not seeing Lil Scott. Once I was guilty of the ticket, I had the prison officer, Ms. R, to mail my letter out for me. She gave me a long speech about how segregation wasn't worth the trouble it would cause to my time. She would come to check on me daily and say, *'Hey Girl!'* I spent the remainder of my time in segregation writing some of my book and figuring out how I was going to navigate through the rest of my bid peacefully and productively.

CHAPTER TWENTY

The prison had incorporated a program called *One Day With God Camp.* It was the biggest day of the year in prison. For the last couple of months, I had been preparing myself for this special day. It was one day that inmates got to spend six hours of leisure with their child(ren). There were prison officers there, but they didn't bother you. In order to participate, you had to have six months of clear conduct, so I made sure that I stayed focused.

Since being incarcerated, this would be the first time that I would get to spend one on one time with Lil Scott. It was exciting because I could play with him and kiss his face without restrictions. Aunt Meka brought Lil Scott to the visit and waited in the car for him until it was over.

"Mommyyy!" Lil Scott said as he ran and jumped in my arms.

"Hey baby! You are getting bigger and bigger every time I see you!" I exclaimed as I covered him in a so many kisses. We ate, had ice cream and cake, and played so many games that we tired ourselves out. I laid out a blanket for us to lay down on and relax while we conversed. "I love you. You know that, right?" I said to him.

"Yes, I love you too. . . more than anything in this whole world. I can't wait for you to come home with me." He responded and tears well in my eyes.

"Aww. I can't wait either baby. What are some things you want to do once I come home with you?" I asked.

"Ummmm." He thought. "I want you to come to my soccer game."

"I will. I'll be at every game. Do you enjoy playing soccer?"

"Yes, and I want to live with you." He exclaimed.

"For sure."

"I want to have my own room."

"Alright. What else?"

"Ummm." He took a second to think. "I want to meet more of our family."

"Oh, you will. Everybody is going to know my baby." I said as I tickled him.

"Why do you have to live here? Why can't you come home with me now?" Lil Scott asked me inquisitively while lying in my arms. I took a few seconds and pondered his question before answering.

"In life there are good choices and bad choices. Mommy made a bad choice and that's why I have to stay here for a while. If I could go back and change it, I would have made better choices. But that's the thing about bad choices. Sometimes there is no way to fix a bad choice and you have to accept the consequences. That's why I want you to strive to always make good choices because good choices come with rewards. Rewards are amazing and make you feel good. Do you understand what I'm saying?"

"Yes. I'm going to make you proud Mommy."

"I'm already proud of you." I said and we laid there in silence for a little. "What color would you like your room?" Lil Scott didn't respond. When I looked down at him, he was fast asleep in my arms, and I realized that this was the first time that I held him since he was a baby. It made me feel good to be his mom and reminded me that I would be able to have more of these moments.

CHAPTER TWENTY-ONE

"Sims." A female counselor called out to me while I was making a cook up.

"Yes?" I asked confused as to what she wanted with me.

"Pack up. You're moving."

"Moving where?" I asked with an attitude no longer paying attention to my food.

"You'll see when you pack up." When I was moved to the west wing of the prison, I was disgusted and upset. I did not want to go over there at all. Large numbers of people were getting sick from staying over there. The toilets were inside the rooms. They painted the walls without cleaning the feces, urine, vomit, and mold off them. It was just nasty. When I got there, I was grateful to have a clean bunky, and to my surprise, Ms. M was one of the main prison officers on that side. She still worked first shift and I still said good morning to her every morning. Until one morning I was still sleep and kind of depressed from missing Lil Scott.

"Sims!" Ms. M called out during rounds. I heard her but I didn't respond. "Sims!" Silence. She came into my room. "Good morning, Sims."

"Good morning, Ms. M." I said flatly.

"Okay. Had to make sure you were okay in here."

"Yes ma'am. I'm okay. Just a little down today. Missing my son."

"It's okay. I know it's depressing being away from your loved ones but don't stay stuck in that depression. Let your son motivate you to do everything you can to get out of here as soon you possibly can."

"Yes ma'am. I am." I smiled. So that I didn't spend my entire day in bed, I went in the TV room before shift change.

It was tradition that when inmates came to prison, they would talk us to death about their life and what could've and should've been. They would share photos of their family. In prison, you could be anything you wanted to be. Some of the crackheads was bosses, most of the boosters were millionaires, and the strippers won world championships in dance battles. I swear I couldn't make up these stories, but I listened to pass time and for entertainment.

Dale was an inmate who was new to prison. We laughed, talked about her memories from the streets, and loved ones. She was about 20 years older than me, but she was very down earth, so we conversed whenever we crossed paths. One night after I came from my job as a tutor, I sat in the TV room which was packed. I talked, joked, laughed, and started playing like I was about to fight some of the inmates.

"What if I was fighting somebody for real? Do you got my back?" I asked Dale.

"Yes. I will always have your back." Dale responded sincerely. We never said it officially, but we became an item that day. We talked and were together every day after that. Eventually, Dale wanted me to quit my job as a tutor and she would just give me the money they paid me so that we could hang out more. Dale had a lot of money, but I loved my job, so I didn't take her up on her offer.

While I declined the offer and kept my job as a tutor, I ended up losing my job anyway by helping my Aunt Christine, my grandmother's sister, on a callout. She had asked me to put her on a callout so that she can visit her friend that was on another side of the prison who was grieving the death of one of her loved ones. A prison guard spotted Aunt Christine on her way over and asked if the officer at the school if Bush, her last name, was requested on a callout and the school prison officer said no. The school officer also removed me from my assignment. After that, me and Dale hung out every day, all day.

"I'll do whatever for you." Dale said to me one day while we walked the yard. She had no idea how many people had said that to me, so I didn't believe people's words. I believe their actions. "Come go to the phone with me." I obliged. She called a man named Hector and told him that she was giving me his number and that whenever I called and asked to do something, for him to do it. Dale then handed me the phone.

"Hello." I spoke.

"Hello Domo. Is there anything I can do for you now?" Hector asked.

"Yes. Send my son an arcade style basketball hoop." I said with ease. Lil Scott had mentioned that he wanted one in one of recent conversations.

"Is that all?" He asked.

"Yes, that's all."

"Where should I send it to?" After giving him Lil Scott's grandmother's information, we hung up. The next day, I woke up with money on my account. Dale showed me that she was exactly who she said she was, and I admired that.

Over the next few weeks, there was a lot of drama going on in our unit. They moved a new stud in. All the women were losing their minds over her. Today we had an off-brand officer and her girlfriend who didn't stay in our unit, snuck in. The girls in the unit were being very messy and somebody went and told the officer. After they took her to seg, the stud went and beat up the girl she was sleeping with in the unit so that she could get sent to seg with her girlfriend.

"Have you ever sex with a woman before?" Out of nowhere Dale asked me while we made a cook up.

"Yes, earlier in my bid." I admitted. I knew why she asked. The sexual attraction was obvious. Since an off-brand officer working that was already distracted with all the commotion, I asked my homegirls to chalk for us. Chalking was a prison term used in regard to where an inmate would watch the officers.

"Are you sure about this?" Dale asked as we snuck back to the room. She was so nervous because she didn't want us to get caught.

"Chill. I got this." It was a bunk bed in the room, so I laid on the top bunk while she gave me head – and listen, the head was good.

After that, we spent even more time together. When her commissary orders came in, she would sneak it up the hallway to my room. Everyone talked about us being together because of the big age difference but we were happy, so it didn't matter what they said. We even talked about being together on the outside when I got home. Dale had an out date as well and hers was before mine. Her family had grown fond of me. One day I got a card in the mail from Dale's mom that read: *Stay strong beautiful. Everyone is looking forward to meeting you when you get home.* I thought that was so sweet. They became like a second family to me.

Dale loved watching me play basketball in the yard. I was still a beast on the court. Everyone was fascinated by my femineity compared the studs that I played ball with. While playing one day, I fell and hit my head hard, so we went inside. I didn't feel like I was in severe pain, so I chose not to go to healthcare immediately. While in the TV room, I felt light-headed suddenly.

"I don't feel well." I said to Dale. "I need to go lay down." Dale went and told the prison officer what was going on. The prison officer called health care and told them to come help me immediately.

"Did she take any drugs?" The health care worker asked.

"No, she didn't take any drugs. She's not that type of inmate." The prison office said in my defense. I ended up in the infirmary for over a week with a concussion. My first night there, the lieutenant came to see me.

"Hey Ms. Sims. Call your mom and tell her to stop calling up here. She done called a hundred times and your sister, Nyesha too. Please call them in the morning." The infirmary porters would sneak me mail and snacks from Cyp, Chrissy, Kat, Chris, Chanika, and Dale. They were all so worried about me, but I was feeling much better. After my accident, I was put on a psychotropic drug that was used to prevent headaches. I would pretend to take the pills so that I could sell them for $5.00 to other inmates as my dad warned me to never take them. That was a way I used to make extra money.

CHAPTER TWENTY-TWO

When I found out that I was getting released from the infirmary, I sent Ms. Hall a message. She moved another inmate out so that she could move me back to Unit 4. Everyone was so happy to see me. They cooked me a lot of food and made sure I had a spot in the shower and the phone line. The next day, we were sitting in the day, talking and chilling, while the prison officer was doing her rounds. The prison officer knocked on an inmate's door that had a sheet up to her window but there was no answer. She knocked again, still no answer.

"I'm opening the door." The prison officer announced before she unlocked the door. She unlocked the door and attempted to open it, but there was a desk pushed against the door blocking. "Officers needed in Unit 4. Possible Code 10!" Officers came running from everywhere. The men prison officers came in from the yard to assist with opening the door, but the inmate had her desk up against the door and her body was hanging behind the desk. Once they saw the inmate hanging, they worked harder to get the door open. Once they got it open enough for a smaller officer to fit, she slipped in the room and attempted to hold the inmate up while kicking the desk out of the way. The prison officer called the code over the intercom and requested assistance.

"There is no movement. All inmates must remain where they are until further notice. I repeat there is a no movement. All inmates must remain where they are until further notice." The sergeant announced over the intercom, so we had to stay there and witness it. They cut her down and laid her body in the hallway as they repeatedly performed CPR on her lifeless body. The paramedics arrived and declared her deceased and covered her with a white sheet. Everyone in a cell had to lock in and everyone out like us had to go to the yard until the coroner came to get her body. We all stared down the hallway as the officers continued to yell at us.

Every single person there was sad, even the prison officers. In that moment, there was a camaraderie formed between the inmates. The friends of the inmate who had hung herself were crying uncontrollably while others consoled them. Closing my eyes, I said a silent prayer for her family and her kids. It was so sad but what's even sadder is that was the first one of many while I was there.

"How are you, Sims?" Ms. M asked as she did her rounds.

"I've been better. Yesterday was a lot."

"I know. You stay strong and out of trouble."

"Yes ma'am." I responded but I didn't really know about staying out of trouble because I had been hearing that there were women in the jail trying to get with D. hey saw how she took care of me and wanted a piece for themselves. I wasn't having it. I approached her about it, and she was honest. She let me know that Sara had been sending her letters but asked me not to say anything to Sara. Okay! Sarcastically, I thought to myself.

I was sitting at the table playing cards with L.G, an inmate I was cool with, when Sara approached our table.

"Domo, do you have a bagel?" She had the audacity to ask me.

"Yes, I have a bagel." I responded and smiled. "I'll bring it to your room."

"Bitches have the nerve to ask me for a bagel knowing that she's been sneaking letters to D." I said to Leslie when Sara walked away.

"What?!" Leslie was shocked.

"Girl, yes! And have the nerve to ask me for a fucking bagel. I got a bagel for her ass." I started taking off my jewelry. "Hold this!"

"Don't put your hands on that girl!" L.G. said but I wasn't paying her no mind.

"Don't tell me what to do. Hold my jewelry." I asked Tiki to chalk while I went down the hallway. Tiki distracted the prison officer by acting like she had a pressing concern while I walked pass. When I got to Sara's room, I immediately started covering up my friend Zoe's stuff who was Sara's bunky.

"What are you doing? Where's the bagel?" Sara asked but I continued to cover Zoe's things. I peeked in the hallway to make sure it was clear.

"Why the fuck are you writing Dale?" I asked.

"Huh? No! It wasn't me." She responded in fear. Fear didn't save her. I beat her ass.

"Stay the fuck away from Dale!" I said while choking her. "Do you understand me?"

"Yes." She said as she struggled for air until I let her go. Walking back to my table to finish my card game, I winked at Tiki on the way back to let her know I was good. A little after I sat down and was back into my card game, the prison officer got up and went towards the hallway near Sara's room. Someone must have dropped a kite on the officer's station that there was a fight on the unit, but they never figured out it was me. When I got back to the day room, NuNu came up to me and asked me what's going on while tying up her hair. NuNu was Dale's prison sister, but we had grown close to be like sisters as well.

Valentine's day came around fast, and Dale made it so special. First, I woke up to a big bag of caramel popcorn, a gold chain, and a diamond ring. The surprises didn't stop there. She had 12 different people deliver me flowers and each had a different message: *Thinking About You, You Are Beautiful, You Are Smart, Lil Scott Loves You, You're Going To Get Through This Time, Etc.* Needless to say, we were locked in.

CHAPTER TWENTY-THREE

Ms. M and I had grown closer. She still made her initial rounds at 6am, but one morning, I noticed it was 6:17am and she hadn't made rounds on my unit yet. When the prison officer came to make rounds in her place, I asked her where Ms. M was.

"She's going to be off for a while." She responded with no further explanation for her absence. I was concerned and worried about her.

Later on, that day, when the walks opened, I went outside in the yard to find Officer J. He informed that Ms. M's daughter had passed away. My heart ached for her, and I was so sad. I couldn't imagine the pain she was enduring from the loss of her child. After she didn't return for a week, I felt like she was never coming back. Until one morning, I heard her keys when she hit the floor. I jumped up and ran to my room door. When she got to my cell, we just stared at one another until tears welled in her eyes.

"I'm so sorry that you are going through this." I started. "Why are you here at work? It's not too soon for you?" I asked concerned.

"Being here is the only thing that keeps me going." She said fighting her tears. Our bond grew even closer over the years. Well, as close as any prison officer could get to an inmate without crossing any lines. She always remained professional.

While walking pass the officer's station, I overheard two prison officers talking about how it was about to be a big shift and officers were being moved around. The next day Ms. M was working a different unit and I was upset about it. I snuck over to the unit to see her.

"Why did they change your unit?"

"They didn't. It was my day off and I picked up this shift. I'll be back on your unit tomorrow." She assured me. While we were talking, another prison officer asked me for my ID and saw that I was out of bounds. He wrote me three tickets before escorting me back to my unit. Ms. M and another prison officer she was cool with helped me beat those tickets.

One time, she worked the day shift, and I don't know if she was upset about it or just having a bad day, but she came in screaming and hollering at everyone. She made everyone get up and pack their rooms up. Inmates were coming to me left and right asking me to get her but there was nothing I could do. She was in her element.

"Can you please get her?" My friend Kathy begged me. "There's a lighter in my room and I don't want to get sent to seg."

"Well, get it out now!" I said confused.

"She's in my room right now and not allowing me to go in. Please go get her." Kathy pleaded. I made my way to Kathy's room.

"What are you doing lady?" I asked Ms. M in an attempt to divert her attention.

"Cleaning this nasty ass room! I have been telling her for a week to clean it, and did she?" She paused and looked at me. "No, she didn't so now I'm going to do it."

"You are hot and sweating. You need to take a break before you overdo it. Besides, it looks so messy in here."

"Exactly the reason I'm cleaning it." She said. Just when I thought there was no hope left, I realized it was time for shift change.

"It's end of shift. Let her clean this mess up herself." I suggested. She looked at her watch and realized I was right.

"Okay. Okay. Now, get your behind in there and clean the rest!" She yelled at Kathy.

"Yes ma'am!" Kathy replied relieved. Everyone laughed and was telling me how I was the only one that could get her to cool off.

After shift change, NuNu came in from work. She had been working in the kitchen for months now. She sent me a message to come up to the day room with my bowl. When I got up there, she had stolen a lot of butter, pizza dough, bell peppers, and onions. We were planning to have a party and NuNu was getting us all of the stuff for pizza and nachos out of the kitchen. Working in the kitchen was a way that people were able to hustle and make some money because they had access to stuff that we couldn't normally get. After we repackaged all the stuff to conceal it as prison bought items, we were still sitting in the day room, when a prison officer came up to me and let me know that I had a visit. Immediately, I jumped up and asked NuNu to help me get prepared. After I picked out my clothes, NuNu ironed my clothes, while I curled my hair. Once I got to the visiting room, I was surprised to see it was my dad as I hadn't seen him in over 10 years. My dad stayed about an hour, but we didn't talk much, because we were both so emotional the entire visit.

CHAPTER TWENTY-FOUR

Dale called me up to the day room and I wasn't sure what it was about, but I made my way there. She was sitting down but when I came in, she jumped up and hugged me.

"I was approved for parole!" She exclaimed excitedly.

"Yesss!" I said happily. I was happy for her but a part of me was sad that she was leaving. I had grown accustomed to us being together daily. Above the romance, she was my friend and truly had my back. I was going to miss that.

"You know I'm still going to be there for you right?"

"Yes, I know that. I'm just going to miss you. That's all." I said.

"Awww! I'm going to miss you too but I'm going to be there for you and I'm going to make sure that Lil Scott is good too."

"For sure." I put my feelings aside and basked in her excitement with her. Everything that she had, she left for me. When the day came for her to leave, I walked her to the gate, and we hugged. She told me to call her after count and I did.

"I want you to stay strong and let me know if anybody fucks with you in here."

"Don't worry about me in here. If I don't know how to do nothing else, I know how to do time. I can handle myself. I want you to be happy and chase your dreams out there." I responded. We chatted about twenty minutes longer.

After our conversation, I went to my room to get my cup so that I could get some ice water before we had to lock up. When I came back on the base area, there was a lot of commotion on the upper level. Before the officer could respond, a big fight had broken out in front of me. I saw Lakeisha spit a blade out of her mouth and start cutting the girls they were fighting. It was blood everywhere. The officer responded by pulling out her mace and spraying everybody on the unit; including people who weren't even involved in the fight. The mace burned our eyes and throats. I was choking, coughing, and throwing up. Later, we found out that Lakeisha cut the girl she was fighting in her face. After that incident, it felt like the entire unit was gloomy, so I stayed in my room mostly. My time started to get to me and at this point, I really felt like giving up. One day, I put my door cover up, turned on my gospel music, and sat behind the door praying and asking God for help and strength. I didn't know how I was going to make it through the rest of this time. Ms. Hall knocked on the door as she did her rounds and asked me was I okay.

"Yes!" I yelled out from behind the door. I got up and washed my face as I collected my thoughts. There were people whose situations were a lot worse than mine, and I knew that I was going to be okay.

One day, my homegirl Fe came to my room and asked me to walk the track with her so I could get out of my room, and I obliged. Fe and I conversed about a young girl that was being taken advantage of by an older inmate. After being incarcerated so long, we both knew that there were some things you just had to get used to, but this wasn't one of those things. We were going for it so over the next few days, we developed our program, Girls Loving Our Wisdom (GLOW). Fe wrote up the paperwork and I reviewed it and confirmed. We submitted the program request and asked for our meetings to be on Fridays at 5p-7p. Our requests were approved, and we were now facilitators of our own program.

GLOW was a mentoring program for younger inmates. We acted as big sisters/mentors to the young girls coming in the facility. We didn't want them to become victims of this vicious cycle. We wanted them to understand that being young and having a second chance was a good thing. We would often speak to them and explain the ramifications of being in prison. It made me feel so good that I could help them in that way as I saw a reflection of myself in them. I was lucky when I came in and had someone to give me the game.

"If you can survive prison, you can survive anything. It's mind over matter. These are some of Michigan's most vicious women. Don't let them manipulate you into spending the rest of your life in prison. Pay attention to your surroundings and always stay ten steps ahead. Don't let this shit eat you alive." An old-timer named Jackie schooled me.

My desire was to pay it forward and I did. It was refreshing to watch them navigate through prison with a new mindset. It was also arranged so that when any of the girls we mentored were going through something, they would place me of Fe on a callout to go talk to them. Most of the prison officers loved GLOW and would call me and Fe to the programs building to converse about ideas to enhance the program. GLOW was special to me. It made me feel like I was beginning to find my purpose.

One day after leaving the Programs Building, I was walking by the blind spot and Officer J happened to be standing there. He grabbed me by my hand and pulled me close to him. I looked at him confused.

"What's up? You been flirting with me for years. You ain't bringing us no money or dropping a bag. So . . ." I asked. Officer J was fine as hell, but I had never been involved with an officer and never planned to. Had I ever decided to, my son and I were definitely going to benefit from it.

CHAPTER TWENTY-FIVE

January 9, 2012

There was a bad feeling in the pit of my stomach when I woke up, so I instantly said a prayer for me, my family, and my case. Then, I got up to shower. When I got out the shower, I went into the TV room and started chilling with Gigi and Kathy. D was Kathy's prison mom so that's how we met.

"Y'all coming outside today, right?" Kathy asked.

"Naww. I don't want to go outside. I'm going to chill right here." I responded.

"Come on please. Me and my girlfriend are getting married today and I want you to stand in for D." Kathy pleaded so I obliged. Since there was only 10 minutes before they called yard, I ran to my room to get my jacket and made in back in time to go outside. There was a lot of people that came to Kima's wedding.

"Come on. Let's walk the track. Y'all know Ms. H is on shift and will come over here cussing us out for us being all together." I said to the crowd after the wedding was over. There were only supposed to be groups of four individuals maximum gathered in one area any given time. Any gatherings with more individuals are subject to everyone getting a ticket. Sure enough, as soon as I finished saying it, Ms. H was already on her way over to us, yelling.

"Ladies, y'all need to keep it moving! I said, Ladies keep it moving." She yelled directly to us.

'Girlll, do your hair.' 'You are miserable.' 'What you ain't get no dick last night?' Different obscenities were yelled at Ms. H from the crowd, and we attempted to start dispersing.

"What did you say Sims?" Ms. H asked and I hadn't said a word to her.

"Why would you call my name out of all people?" I asked irritated.

"Because I know your smart-ass mouth and you're the ring-leader."

"Nahhh It's a new year. I'm trying to start it off on a good foot and here you go being messy."

"Messy?" She said offended. "Messy was you and your Momma in prison together." She smiled. "Yeah, remember when your crackhead ass mother was here?"

"What the fuck does my mother being a crackhead have to do with you? Huh?" I asked and stepped towards her. By this time, she was standing on the table we were all just gathered at. "Because on your best day, you couldn't fuck with my mother on her worst day." She jumped down off the table and started coming towards me. "Girl, you better not touch me." I warned her.

'Write her ass up!' 'Write a grievance!' 'Write her up Domo!' Everyone started shouting as Ms. H & I stood face to face.

"I ain't losing my job for you. I got something for you bitch." Ms. H said before running towards the field house.

"I bet this bitch is about to send me to seg." I said out loud as I ran towards the gate.

"You know all inmates go in at the same time." The prison officer stopped.

"I have to go to the bathroom. I just came on my period." I don't know if it was adrenaline or my need to make it seem like an authentic emergency, but I rocked back and forth a bit. He looked at me skeptical at first before allowing me to go inside. Making my way to my room quickly, I gathered all of my contraband and gave it to my bunk buddy.

"What's going on?" She asked me.

"I'm about to go to seg. I don't have a lot of time. Make sure Chrissy gets this." I said as I wrote down Grandma's phone number. "This is my grandmother's number. If I get sent to seg call her and let her know."

"Okay, I got you. What about your stuff?" She asked.

"Damn." I had to think fast. We were only allowed two pair of shoes, but I had eight pair of shoes. I gave her a pair to hold the other 5 pair for me. After we got everything arranged, the intercom sounded.

Sims to the officers' station! Sims to the officers' station! After I got everything situated, I made my way to the officers' station.

"What's going on?" Ms. S, the prison counselor, asked me. I told her my side of what happened. "I would need statements from others who witnessed what you're saying. As of right now, it's out of my hands because the sergeant has already ordered you to segregation." Inmates started coming from outside as Ms. H and five other prison officers ran in the unit to cuff me.

'It's your fault that she's going to the hole!' 'You know you ain't right H!' 'You started it so how are you locking her up?' 'Get your hands off of her.' 'Get your fucking hands off of her!' The inmates shouted outraged. They squeezed my cuffs as tight as they could.

"Ms. S, they cuffed me too tight!" I called out to her, but Ms. H yanked by my arm towards her and pushed me through the door. The inmates erupted in in outbursts again. When we got to segregation, there was no more room, so they took me to level 4 side of the prison. Everyone was yelling out of their cells to me. *'Domo! Domo! What happened? Why are you going seg?'* I didn't answer because I was so mad that I was even there. I went to my hearing a few days later and was found guilty. They dropped my charge for threatening behavior which is a major misconduct and found me guilty of an insolent which is a minor misconduct. Basically, it was a charge for saying things I shouldn't have to an officer. I spent ten days in the hole. While I was there, everyone was sending me letters and messages, but NuNu pulled off sending me a bagel sandwich and some chips.

"Domo! Domo! Why you in seg?" Officer T asked as she banged on my door, and everyone laughed at her calling me by my nickname. She was really childish, but I appreciated her for always making light of the situations at hand in order to put a smile on an inmate's face.

CHAPTER TWENTY-SIX

When I got out, I knew I wouldn't have the same bunky, but I was hoping that I didn't have a nasty one. They moved me to the east wing of the prison and when I got to my room, I was pleasantly surprised.

"Girl, every time you get out the hole, you are sent to be my bunky!" Ms. Bernice said with a chuckle. She wasn't lying either. Ms. Bernice was an older lady that I had shared a room with the last time I was released from segregation. They brought me my belongings, so I talked to Ms. Bernice ad I went through my stuff. Most of it was gone and I didn't have any food at all. That irritated me. Officers always throwing away people's food, trying to be funny.

"I'm boutta take a shower and clean up, Ms. Bernice. I'll see you in a bit."

"Okay. Stay out of trouble, hear?" Ms. Bernice advised.

"Yes ma'am." After I took my shower and got cleaned up, I wrote Cyp a letter and sent it asking her to meet me at breakfast then I went to sleep. The next morning, I went to breakfast and waited for her to show. When her unit was called, I saw her come in. Her eyes scanned the room until they landed on me, and she made her way over. "I wrote you a letter. I didn't know if you were going to come."

"You knew I was coming as soon as I heard you were out. Do you need anything?"

"I don't have any food."

"Okay. That's it? Send somebody to lunch." Cyp always had my back. This time was no different. When I went back to my unit, I asked an inmate I knew from the west side of the prison if I could pay her $20 to meet Cyp at lunch and smuggle my food to me. She agreed. After lunch she bought me my food and a letter from Cyp. She always trying to tell me to let her whenever I needed anything. For the most part, I tried to work hard or hustle for anything that I needed. For damn sure, there were times when I just went without; especially when it came to making sacrifices for my son. I was appreciative for what I had and didn't bother her too much. I made to call Lil Scott and Grandma before locking up for the night. My conversation with Lil Scott made me miss him so much. Lil Scott had so much to talk to me about.

"Mom, I couldn't wait for you to call!" Lil Scott said as he answered the phone. This made my heart smile. Lil Scott was telling on everybody because he knew I would believe everything he told me. He was so full of life and gave me every reason to continue to press forward.

Soon after that, I went on a callout to see Ms. C in the programs building to introduce her to the idea of having a Boy Scouts program partnered with the prison so that Moms could see their sons.

"I think that's an amazing idea, so I'll tell you what. I'll give you their contact information and you can write them to share your idea with them. If they agree to send a representative to coordinate and oversee the program, I will work on getting it approved."

"Thank you so much. Ms. C. By the way, I love this office. I want to work over here." I said seriously.

"Ms. Sims, the waiting list is long but go ahead and apply." She laughed.

As soon as I got back to my room, I wrote the letter to Boy Scouts of America. A few weeks later, two men agreed to volunteer their time from of Boys Scouts of America. This was truly a blessing. For the first time in prison history, we were afforded the opportunity to build strong bonds with our sons in hopes of creating a lifetime of security and confidence in them. Ms. A, who also worked in the programs building, was able to get the two men approved and Ms. C was able to get the program approved so that the visits would occur every month.

All of the girls' participation in the program was predicated on influencing their sons to become responsible, independent young men in order to serve a worthy purpose in society. Unfortunately for some of us, our realities weren't the same. A couple of the girls were doing life, and this saddened me because I would continue these efforts with my son beyond my incarceration. I was so excited and couldn't wait to call home and tell Lil Scott.

"But I always come see you Ma."

"These visits will be different. Aunt Meka and Grandma won't be at this visit. It'll just be me and you." I informed him. He was excited and so was I. I loved that he enjoyed spending time with me just the two of us. After speaking with him, I called Aunt Meka and let her know about the Boy Scouts visits and she promised that she would do her best to get Lil Scott to every visit.

Grandma and Aunt Meka brought Lil Scott for the Boys Scout visit, and it went amazing. It was February so the coordinators organized for us to a Black History Month activity where we discussed great black history leaders and learned information about them. After the activity, the moms were able to just spend time with their sons. We talked about school, shoes, soccer, and basketball. I couldn't wait to go to one of his games. While conversing, I noticed that he had patches of dry skin and I felt one on his ear. *This baby didn't stand a chance. Big Scott and I both suffered from eczema.* I thought to myself. I made a mental note to tell his grandmother the name of a cream to get his doctor to prescribe him. It worked for me. The visit came to an end, and I had mixed emotions. I was sad anytime I had to part from Lil Scott, but I was also looking forward to the next one. I blew Lil Scott more kisses than I gave him as he was leaving the room.

"Sims, you can stay seated. You have another visit." The prison guard said as he dismissed the inmates back to their units.

"Can I run to the bathroom real quick?" I asked and the prison guard allowed me to. I ran to my room and squirted a little of my cream on my finger. When I got back, I waited for Grandma, Aunt Meka, Ny, and Lil Scott to come in. When I hugged him, I snuck and rubbed the cream on the dry patch I felt on his ear. My visit with my family was enjoyable as well. My heart was full that day. We laughed, ate, and played card games. Grandma caught me up on all the family gossip. *Nye did this. . . Cranston and Lonzo went here. . . Donnie this. . . Your dad called me. . . I ran into. .*

.Etc. She sure had a good memory. On the way out, she made sure to remind me to call her later.

The first Boys Scout visit was a complete success. It was organized and set up very nicely. We found out that we could eat Subway at every visit. There was eight moms and thirteen sons. The joy that radiated in that room was unexplainable, but I know for sure that program made a difference in the lives of the moms and their sons. The prison staff was impressed and proud of me for how I made motherhood a priority despite my circumstances. Three months later, Ms. C was calling me to her office for an interview and I was hired as a Programs Clerk in the programs building.

"Well, how you pull this off Domo?" Ms. C asked as I entered her office.

"It ain't what you know. It's who you know." I said jokingly.

CHAPTER TWENTY-SEVEN

"Domo! Domo!" I heard someone calling my name while I was taking a nap. If it's one thing I hate, it's being awakened from my sleep, and everybody knew that.

"What?" I yelled as I got up.

"I have a letter for you." They responded. When I got the letter, immediately, I noticed my mother's handwriting. Instantly, I was sad. I hated that she was back in prison. She informed me that she was sentenced to 18 months. I knew I had to send her some stuff, so I gathered what I had and sent Cyp and Chrissy a letter to meet me at lunch.

"My mom is back, and I need to send her some stuff." I told Cyp when we met at lunch.

"Okay. We got you. We'll send her some stuff too. Send somebody out to the night yard." Cyp replied. When I returned to my unit, I sent the same lady who I had paid before. When she came in, she had so much stuff for my mom from them. The next day, I got an RG&C Porter to take my mom the stuff and a letter from me.

My mom and I met on callouts to church. We would meet on the walkway and walk really slow to church so that we could talk. She would tell me how much she loved me. As we approached the west side, where church was, we would show them our itinerary and take our seats. Before I sat down with my mom, me and Blue praise danced like we usually did in church on Sundays. Together, we led the praise dance team for several years and we met three times a week for rehearsal. For me, praise dance was an out of prison experience. During our rehearsals, we laughed, prayed, talked, and always snuck some food in the gym. During church, my mom and I would write letters back and forth because they would put you out over talking.

Mom: I can't wait for you to come home. I know when you get home things will be different. I am going to have Will send us some money (her husband). I love you and I am proud of you. You are so beautiful.

Me: I don't like to see you in prison. You don't need to be here. Just let me do my time. I don't be really having stuff. I be having to just make things happen.

Mom: I promise that when I get out this time, I am going to be there for you. I will send you money and cards.

Me: I can do the time. It's just hard being away from Lil. Scott. I'm ready to go home. I have to be strong but some days I'm just not strong. I will be praying for you. I just want you to do better.

My mother and I grew closer during that her bid that time. One thing that came out of the time we shared incarcerated that was special to me was that we got to experience One Day With God Camp together. Not only would I see Lil Scott but for the first time, I would get to meet my little brother, Chance, that my mom had while she was incarcerated. Everyone around me was happy for me, including the prison officers, but I was nervous. I wanted our first impression to be good of each other.

My mom and I were the first Mother/Daughter inmates in the One Day With God camp, and I was the first inmate to meet their sibling in the camp's history. The camp was designed for the mothers and their sons to spend time together, but the program staff and the warden made special accommodations for me, Lil Scott, my mom, and Chance. That way I could spend time with Chance and my mom could spend time with Lil Scott as well.

"Sister, you are so pretty." Chance said initially when meeting me and it warmed my heart. We spent the six hours we had playing games, talking, and spending time getting to know one another.

"Ma, is this your first time meeting Chance?" Lil Scott asked.

"Yes, it is baby, but I hope it's not the last time Chance. I would love to be able to see you and spend time with you when I come home. Is that okay?" I asked.

"Yes. Come see me anytime." Chance replied and we both smiled.

"Domo!" Snoop called out to me from the door. I snuck over get the t-shirt, towel, and socks that I had someone paint for me. When I returned, I stuffed it in his book bag and told him not to tell anyone he had it until he got home. When the day ended, we all hugged and left filled up. When I walked out the field house, Officer J was out there.

"Sims, come here." He demanded. *He is so damn fine.* I thought to myself.

"What's the word J?" I responded.

"Nothing. How was your day?"

"It was good."

"Oh okay. That's what's up. I saw all those kids up in there. You coming back to the field house tonight on your call out?"

"Who's working in here?" I asked.

"Me. Duh."

"Of course." I smiled. "Yeah, I'll be back."

"Make sure you come back. I got something for you." He said as I walked off. When I walked in the unit, my prison kid, B, handed me a letter from Kat.

CHAPTER TWENTY-EIGHT

The issues with the youth at the prison didn't stop but Fe and I had been very successful with education and intervention. Sometimes, no matter how much of a good person you are, there are some prison staff members who will look at you as nothing more than an animal. One day, a staff member of that kind sat in on a GLOW session and decided that she didn't like how it was being ran. As a result, the program was discontinued. I was saddened by this, but there were so many young girls that we had put in position to make better decisions for themselves while in prison. We had done a lot for them as a result of starting GLOW.

By the time of the termination of GLOW, I had also joined the National Lifers Association (NLA) and I was the chair of the youth committee. At a Warden Forum Meeting, we asked for a separate housing unit just for the youth so that it could maximize their safety and sanity. The warden denied our request, saying there was no room for it. We were passionate about helping the youth, so we didn't let the denial stop us.

There was a staff member, Ms. J, whom also had the passion to help the youth. We gave her our idea about the housing unit for the youth and asked her to present it as her own. Recognition wasn't our goal, change was. Our goal was to have safe living conditions for the youth.

"What should be the name?" Ms. J asked.

"We don't really care about the name. We just want them safe." I responded.

She presented it and it was approved. In fact, they thought it was a brilliant idea. The program was ultimately named the Youth Enrichment Program. I was still working as a Programs Clerk when one day, I asked Ms. Mac, a programs building staff member, that I wanted I would like to volunteer as a mentor in the Youth Enrichment Program. She loved the idea and promised that she would get me over there as a volunteer. She kept her promise and as a result, I was moved to their unit in the Calhoun Building. My work there included mentorship, mediated their issues, and did their hair. My residency in the Calhoun Building with the Youth Enrichment Program lasted about four years and a benefit of my role is that I was able to advocate for the youth. My advocation for them and the committees I served contributed greatly to my public speaking skills.

No amount of public speaking could prepare my words for my visit with Grandma. She came to see me and let me know that she had cancer and that she prayed that she lived to see me come home. That put me in a very depressive space where I stayed in bed for days crying. Due to being a member of the group, Chance For Life, I was scheduled to go to a special program where Anthony King spoke to us. Anthony King was a Christian gentleman who was a member of the parole board.

"First, I would like to say that I am so proud of you all." Anthony started his speech, encouraging and speaking life into us. "I am a Christian man. A believer of second chances. Do not get caught and let this system rob you of this second chance. Remember, you have an out date. Nothing and no one are worth pushing that date back. Thank you for having me." He concluded.

"When I go to my parole hearing, I want to go up in front of him." I whispered to my friend, Honey Bun.

Pretty soon after that event, I had become the Chair of the Warden's Forum. It felt amazing to accomplish such a plight. That was the highest position you could have as an inmate. During my time in the role, I was able to advocate for the women of the entire prison. One initiative I'm proud of was introducing the inmate's desire to have media players in the prison and having it approved. That was major because electronics were not allowed in the history of the prison's existence. Though I was proud of my impact in that position, sometimes that pride is worn down by annoyance of the amount of frivolous request from the inmates.

By this time, my mom had her eighteen-month bid and had gone home. More importantly, she kept her word. She sent me money, visited me, brought Lil Scott to see, and answered the phone for me consistently. On one of the visits, the prison officers who knew my mom from when she was incarcerated, were impressed with how well she was doing.

"Tonya? Wow, look at you beautiful. Fly as ever. Girl give me those boots." The prison officer complimented my mom. "Seriously, you look beautiful and I'm glad you're doing well."

"Thank you." My mom responded humbly. She was so pretty, fly, clean, and healthy. I was prouder of her than I'd ever been.

CHAPTER TWENTY-NINE

After the completion of my six-month term as the Chair of the Warden's Forum, my mom had returned to prison to serve one year. This disappointed me significantly, but I didn't tell her. My disappointment didn't stop me from supporting her and making sure she was alright and had everything she needed during her bid. About six months into her bid, she sent me a letter telling me to meet her at dinner. When I arrived at dinner, my mom was already there and seemed to be very upset.

"What's wrong Ma?" I asked concerned as I sat down.

"I've been trying my best to stay to myself and stay out of trouble." She started. "But fuck that. I want to fight!" She replied through clenched teeth.

"Fight? Who? What happened?"

"These bitches on my unit that keep fucking with me!" She said angrily. I could tell it was really bothering her greatly, so I had to act now. My coat was distinct, so I looked around the cafeteria before my eyes landed on an associate of mine. She and I switched jackets so that I could wear her state jacket. I zipped up the jacket and pulled my skully down real low.

When dinner was over, I went out of place to my mother's unit. Out of place refers to going somewhere unassigned or going to a unit other than the one you were housed in without permission. Immediately after arriving on the unit, I started sending for girls that were bothering my mom.

"Tell them bitches come on outside because I want to fight." I said to the girl I sent to get them. While the girls never came out, an old timer, T.S., did come out to speak with me.

"What's going on Domo?" she asked.

"What's going on is it's obviously some bitches on this unit that don't know who the fuck I am because they keep bothering my mom."

"I'll handle it." T.S. responded and she did. The problem was solved right then and there. They never bothered my mom again. At the time, I had resigned as a mentor at the youth building because it had fallen away from what it was designed to be and became messy. As a result, I was moved to the same unit as my mom. Daily, we would meet each other on the back porch, and I would take her food that I cooked for her.

One day, me and my friend Starr went to see the old counselor at the youth program, Ms. H because she had decided to resign from the youth unit. She knew we were coming so she was expecting us. A month later, the inspector called for me.

"Where you going?" Starr asked.

"The inspector called for me so I'm about to go up there and see what they want."

"Oh yeah? Me too. I'm going to go in a second though. I have to do something first." Starr responded. Starr was about to go home, and I didn't involve myself in anything to get myself in trouble, so I was not worried.

"Where were you on February 3rd?" The inspector asked, catching me off guard.

"I don't remember." I responded because I really didn't. My days were pretty much spent the same way; in my room, tv room, in the yard, and the cafeteria the few times I visited there. I still didn't understand the importance or significance of the date.

"Well, let me jog your memory. On February 3rd, you were out of bounds, visiting Ms. H. So, today, you're going to segregation."

"What? She was expecting me. She knew I was coming. Ask her!" Despite my pleas, prison officers were called to cuff me and escort me to segregation. On the walk back, I told a girl that was on Cyp' unit to tell her that I was getting sent to segregation. Also, I saw Starr and told her they were sending us to segregation for being out of place. Starr and I ended up bunk buddies in segregation.

"Somebody hating ass told the inspector that we went to see Ms. H." Starr stated as she paced the floor.

"Hell yeah. Ain't no way they those cameras back that far. They would've been come and got us." I said in response. We spent the next few days getting our story together and the day before our hearing, I told Starr to pray.

"I don't know how to pray." Starr admitted so I prayed out loud for both of us. Despite having our story air-tight and saying a powerful prayer the night before, we were both found guilty at our hearing. We spent a total of 40 days in the hole and remained bunk buddies the entire time.

While on segregation, we were classified as Level 4 inmates, which required the highest security level for inmates. So, we were locked in our down 24 hours a day. Every 10 days, we went to the Security Classification Class (SCC), but they repeatedly denied us for reclassification. The first time we went, the prison officer was on the phone talking to the officer that gave us the ticket during the class. *'Weren't you just the Chair of the Warden's Forum?'* Another prison officer recognized me. It was embarrassing because once you have that high of an achievement, they hate to see you make a mistake. So, everything is intensified when it came to punishment for even the littlest of mistakes.

Our fourth time going to SCC, I was released but Star was denied again. I was moved back to the unit where I could see my mom, so I was happy about that. However, much like other times, after segregation, I had to start over with my stuff. So, I started a 2-for-1 store which became big. About a month after my release from segregation, my mom had run into a problem with another girl.

"What's your problem with my mom?" I asked the girl as I ran down on her.

"I don't owe you no explanation." She said looking me up and down.

"Okay. You right. I got you." I smirked before walking off. One day while I was tying up my hair, I happened to look out the window and saw the girl on the back porch. Without thinking, I ran down there, and we started fighting. After I beat her up, my mom came outside and attempted to fight the girl, but I told her to let it go so that we could disperse and avoid going to segregation. Around the same time, Starr was released from segregation and went home shortly after. My mom went home as well and got back on her feet quickly. Things went back to how they were when she went home before. She answered the phone whenever I called, visited me, and sent me money.

CHAPTER THIRTY

By the time I was down to my last two years, I had started preparing my exit plan and focusing on the things I needed to do in order to be successful at home. Not only was I taking college courses, but I worked as a Clerk in the school building. I had already completed school for Culinary Arts and received my national certification. Also, I had earned my certification as a Mechanic. It was now time for me to request a parole hearing. The counselor who wrote my pre-release evaluation report (PER), wrote it beautifully speaking highly of me. She also instructed me to get letters from my family for my parole request file. Some of the letters I wrote for them and mailed them to them so they could mail them back in to the counselor. Even prison officers had wrote letters for my file. Once my parole request file was complete, the counselor sent it to the parole board. I would visit her office every day.

"Girllll, did they send my parole board hearing date yet?" I would ask.

"Sims, you're getting on my nerves. When they send it, I will deliver it to you personally." She responded one day so I decided to wait patiently for a response. One day before count, she knocked on my door and I just smiled because I knew she was bringing my parole date and time. She handed me a piece of paper that detailed my parole board hearing.

"August 20th at 8:30am! Okay. Okay." I read the dated excitedly.

"Do you want to bring a representative?" She asked.

"Yes."

"Alright. After count, come to my office so we can do the paperwork." She instructed. After talking to the counselor, I ran to Honey Bun's room and let her know my parole board hearing date. I handed her the paper.

"OMG! Anthony King!" Honey Bun shouted, and we jumped up and down together.

"Yesss! God is so good. Thank God!" I praised God. After count, I went to see the counselor and completed the paperwork for Aunt Meka to be my representative. I called my family immediately after leaving her office to give them the new and everyone was so happy.

"My baby made parole y'all!" Grandma yelled to the people in the background. After calling them, I called to inform Lil Scott.

On the day of my parole hearing, I got up very early and prayed. *God, please allow your will to be done.* It was a lot of inmates having their parole hearing the same day, but the counselors allowed the inmates with representatives go first.

"Sims. . .It's your turn." Ms. R, a counselor, called out to me.

"Yes ma'am." I said nervously.

"Listen. Go in there, be yourself, and tell the truth." Ms. R reassured me. When I walked in, I felt even more nervous. Aunt Meka was already seated so I embraced her with a hug before taking a seat myself. The camera was already recording the hearing and Anthony was on the monitor in front of us. The pressure I felt that moment was nostalgic to how I felt during my trial. I simply hoped for the best and prepared for the worst. *I have to get home to my baby.*

"Dominica Sims, we are here today to discuss your parole conditioned release. After serving fifteen calendar years, I've had the chance to review your file. Tell me about your case. How did you find yourself in such an extreme situation at such a young age and how have you grown during your incarceration?" Anthony King started the hearing jumping right in.

"I have had some struggles in my growing up, but I come from a decent background. Looking back, there are some things that I would have done differently. However, I have accomplished and learned a lot during my incarceration. My plan if granted parole is to immediately become active in my son's life, secure meaningful employment, honor my parole, and be a productive membership of society." I concluded after telling him a little about how I ended up in prison.

"In the 15 years that you have been incarcerated, I only see two major misconduct tickets. Can you explain the fighting incident in 2008?" Mr. King asked, and I was honest about what occurred, and we moved pass that. "You have truly made the best of your time here. I see that you have over 100 certificates of completion, a state certification, and a national certification. You have also made great strides in your education and made great use of your time here. That is very impressive."

"Thank you! It was a priority for me to be committed to making the best of my time here. I want to go home to my son as the best version of myself." There was a little small talk before my parole hearing concluded and I thanked him for his time.

"Do you have any questions?" He asked.

"Umm. . . No sir."

"Are you sure that you don't have any questions?"

"No sir. I don't."

"Auntie, do you have any questions?"

"No sir. I don't have any questions, but I would like to thank you for your times and let you know that I am so proud of my niece and the woman she's become. She was young and made a bad decision but has grown so much since then. She didn't let her circumstances stop her from preparing for her future for herself and her son. I'm most certain that she is going to do the right thing when she comes home. She's learned her lesson from her bad decision, and I pray that you grant her the chance to prove herself." Aunt Meka and he thanked her before returning his attention to me.

"Ms. Sims, you don't have any questions for me at all?"

"Huh? Should I Mr. King?"

"You have spent 15 years of your life incarcerated. You are granted a parole hearing and don't wanna know if you're going home?"

"Yes sir. I do want to know."

"So, I ask again. Do you have any questions for me Ms. Sims?"

"Am I going home?"

"My recommendation will be for you to be paroled. However, there are two other votes that are required. Since I conducted your parole hearing, I will have influence over the decision." Thirty days later, I received the letter that I was granted parole. I was super excited, and I immediately went and called Lil Scott who was excited as well. He had already been on the computer looking up my out date with his cousin.

On my last day in prison, Cyp came to see me and wished me well. A lot of the inmates that I had built reports with sent me notes or came to me to give me one final hug. I received a long letter from Ava and made sure before I left that I responded to her letter. On my way out, Ms. Anne was on a ride in coming in again. I hadn't seen her since county. When the gates opened, I was embraced by a lot of my family and friends, and I couldn't be happier to be free. My first day out, I went straight to Lil Scott's basketball game. In that moment, I realized life works in full circle and sometimes that's a good thing. One cycle I prayed to never repeat was incarceration. I was no longer convicted to my pruning process. It was time for this diamond to shine. So, finally I could put this all behind me and begin a new chapter in my life. By the grace of God, I made it home. . .

About the Author

My name is Dominica Sharda Sims. In January 2020 I was released from MDOC (Michigan department of Corrections) after serving a 15-year sentence and I have not looked back. I refused to waste any more time. Throughout my incarceration, I knew that I wanted to share my story and experiences with the world. Through faith, I stepped out on a journey of becoming an author and I did it. I am here to share my story with the world.

Born and raised in Kalamazoo, Michigan I always knew that I had a purpose in life. It would be in my most difficult years that I would find myself. With gratitude and pose I have started to build a meaningful life for my son and myself. In life, I had to learn the hard way. I Learned that everything that glitter ain't gold, the grass isn't always greener on the other side, and if you play with fire, you will get burned. I swallowed big pills and learned the hardest lessons. Through all this I learned that where there is a will there is a way. I learned how to make the best out of any situation, I learned to turn lemons into lemonade, that pressure burst pipes, only the strong survive and as you will see I learned to move with love, integrity, and pure intentions no matter what.

In 2022 I started a mentoring program for young girls in my Kalamazoo Mi. GLOW (Girls Loving Our Wisdom) is a mentoring program that is dedicated to improving the lives, opportunities and situations for at-risk youth in the community. Through my experience I want to help them become the best version of themselves.

Dominica Sharda

Made in United States
North Haven, CT
17 May 2023

36668836R00093